Disability Discrimination Act 1995

Code of Practice

Employment and Occupation

Books are to be returned
the last da...

Disability Rights Commission

London: TSO

First published 2004

ISBN 0 11 703419 3

Printed in the United Kingdom for The Stationery Office

Foreword

This Code of Practice explains how disabled people are protected from discrimination if they are in employment, if they are seeking employment, or if they are involved in a range of occupations. It is one of two Codes of Practice which have been prepared and issued by the Disability Rights Commission to give practical guidance on the operation of Part 2 of the Disability Discrimination Act 1995. The other such Code relates to discrimination by trade organisations and qualifications bodies.

It is pleasing to note that rates of employment among disabled people have risen in recent years as more and more employers have adopted better employment practices. Nevertheless, it is still the case that only about half of those disabled people who are of working age are actually in employment – although many more want to work and are capable of doing so.

Although discrimination against disabled people in employment has been outlawed since the Disability Discrimination Act came into force in 1996, the law has continued to evolve. Not only have the original provisions of the Act been subject to judicial interpretation, but major changes have been made to the legislation itself. As from October 2004 the extent of the Act's coverage is extended significantly to take account of the requirements, so far as they relate to disability discrimination, of an EU Council Directive of 2000, establishing a general framework for equal treatment in employment and occupation. In making these legislative changes Parliament has also signalled the need to further progress the reform agenda on the employment and employability of disabled people, to ensure equality of opportunity.

This Code of Practice sets out our understanding of the law as it applies from October 2004 onwards. While many of the original building blocks of the 1995 Act remain in place, there are some new concepts, and the scope of the legislation has been widened considerably. These changes undoubtedly increase the level of protection for disabled people, but they also add to the complexity of the law. As the Code has been prepared with particular regard to helping lawyers when advising their clients, and to assisting courts and tribunals when interpreting the new concepts, it is necessarily comprehensive and detailed. However, the DRC has also produced a range of other information to help disabled people and employers alike to understand their rights and responsibilities. How to find this information is explained in Appendix C to the Code.

This Code replaces the 'Code of Practice for the elimination of discrimination in the field of employment against disabled persons or persons who have had a disability', issued by the Secretary of State for Education and Employment in 1996.

Bert Massie CBE

Chairman, Disability Rights Commission

Contents

6

7

1 Introduction

Purpose of Part 2 of the Act

1.1 The Disability Discrimination Act 1995 (the Act) brought in measures to prevent discrimination against disabled people. Part 2 of the Act is based on the principle that disabled people should not be discriminated against in employment or when seeking employment. It also protects disabled people engaged in a range of occupations. Employers must comply with the duties set out in Part 2, as must others to whom those duties apply (see paragraphs 3.8 to 3.14).

1.2 Except for the Armed Forces, these duties now apply to all employers no matter how many (or how few) people they employ. The law changed in this regard on 1 October 2004. Other major changes in the law which took effect on that date, including the extension of the duties to some people or bodies who are not employers, are summarised in Appendix A.

Purpose of the Code

1.3 This Code of Practice (the Code) gives practical guidance on how to prevent discrimination against disabled people in employment or when seeking employment. It describes the duties of employers and others in this regard. The Code helps disabled people to understand the law and what they can do if they feel that they have been discriminated against. By encouraging good practice, the Code assists employers to avoid workplace disputes and to work towards the elimination of discrimination against disabled people.

1.4 The Code also gives guidance on the law which is intended to help lawyers when advising their clients, and to assist courts and tribunals when interpreting new legal concepts. The Code explains the operation and effect of technical statutory provisions – some of which only came into force on 1 October 2004, and many of which have a complex legal effect. Because of this, the Code is necessarily comprehensive and detailed. However, the Disability Rights Commission (DRC) also produces a range of other publications about the Act, and about the rights of disabled people under it, which are intended to be of use to a range of audiences and for a variety of purposes. Details of how to obtain these publications are included in Appendix C.

s 53A

1.5 The DRC has prepared and issued this Code under the Act on the basis of a request by the Secretary of State. It applies to England, Wales and Scotland. A similar but separate Code applies to Northern Ireland.

Status of the Code

s 53A(8)

1.6 The Code does not impose legal obligations. Nor is it an authoritative statement of the law – that is a matter for the courts and tribunals. However, the Code can be used in evidence in legal proceedings under the Act. Courts and employment tribunals must take into account any part of the Code that appears to them relevant to any question arising in those proceedings. If employers (and others who have duties under the Act's provisions on employment and occupation) follow the guidance in the Code, it may help to avoid an adverse decision by a court or tribunal in such proceedings.

How to use the Code

1.7 This chapter gives an introduction to the Code. Chapter 2 sets out some general guidance on how to avoid discrimination. Chapter 3 contains an overview of the Act's provisions on employment and occupation, and those provisions are examined in more detail in subsequent chapters.

1.8 Chapter 4 details what is meant by discrimination and harassment, and Chapter 5 explains the duty to make reasonable adjustments for disabled people. Chapter 6 examines the relevance of justification under Part 2. Chapters 7 and 8 consider the application of these principles in the context of recruitment processes and of subsequent employment, and Chapter 9 examines their application to certain occupations.

1.9 Chapter 10 explains how the Act's provisions on employment and occupation operate in the particular context of occupational pension schemes and group insurance services.

1.10 Chapter 11 describes how the Act deals with discrimination in providing employment services. Such services include vocational guidance and training.

1.11 Chapter 12 looks at particular issues concerning adjustments to premises, and Chapter 13 deals with various other points and explains what happens if discrimination is alleged.

1.12 Appendix A summarises some recent changes in the Act's provisions on employment and occupation. Appendix B gives more information on what is meant by 'disability' and by 'disabled person'. Separate statutory guidance relating to the definition of disability has been issued under the Act (see paragraph 3.6). Appendix C lists other sources of relevant information about matters referred to in the Code.

1.13 Each chapter of the Code should be viewed as part of an overall explanation of the Act's provisions on employment and occupation and the regulations made under them. In order to understand the law properly it is necessary to read the Code as a whole. The Code should not be read too narrowly or literally. It is intended to explain the principles of the law, to illustrate how the Act might operate in certain situations and to provide general guidance on good practice. There are some questions which the Code cannot resolve and which must await the authoritative interpretation of the courts and tribunals. The Code is not intended to be a substitute for taking appropriate advice on the legal consequences of particular situations.

Examples in the Code

1.14 Examples of good practice and how the Act is likely to work are given in boxes. They are intended simply to illustrate the principles and concepts used in the legislation and should be read in that light. The examples should not be treated as complete or authoritative statements of the law.

1.15 As stated in paragraph 1.2, the Act's provisions on employment and occupation now apply to small employers as well as to larger ones. The size of an employer is sometimes relevant to the way in which the Act applies. Where this is the case, examples in the Code show how the application of the Act could be affected by the size of the employer.

1.16 While the examples refer to particular situations, they should be understood more widely as demonstrating how the law is likely to be applied generally. They can often be used to test how the law might apply in similar circumstances involving different disabilities or situations. Some of the examples are based on real cases which have been decided by the courts. In general, however, the examples attempt to use as many different varieties of disabilities and situations as possible to demonstrate the breadth and scope of the Act. Examples relating to men or women are given for realism and could, of course, apply to people of either gender.

References to 'employers' in the Code

1.17 Throughout the Code, references are made to 'employers' for convenience. However, as explained in paragraphs 3.11 and 3.12, the Act's provisions on employment and occupation impose obligations on persons who might not ordinarily be described as employers – such as partners in firms, barristers and people providing practical work experience. References in the Code need to be read in this light.

Other references in the Code

1.18 References to the Act are shown in the margins. For example, s 1(1) means section 1(1) of the Act and Sch 1 means Schedule 1 to the Act. References to Part 2, 3 or 4 refer to the relevant Part of the Act. Where reference is made to regulations, the appropriate Statutory Instrument (SI) number is shown in the margin.

Changes to the legislation

1.19 The Code refers to the Disability Discrimination Act as of 1 October 2004. There may be changes to the Act or to other legislation, for example, to the range of people who are considered to be 'disabled' under the Act, which may have an effect on the duties explained in this Code. You will need to ensure that you keep up to date with any developments that affect the Act's provisions. You can get relevant information from the DRC (see below for contact details).

Further information

1.20 Copies of the Act and regulations made under it can be purchased from the Stationery Office (see inside the front of the Code for details). Separate codes covering other aspects of the Act, and guidance relating to the definition of disability are also available from the Stationery Office. The text of all the DRC's codes (including this Code) can also be downloaded free of charge from the DRC website (see paragraph 1.21).

1.21 Free information about the Act is available on the DRC website. It can also be obtained by contacting the DRC Helpline. This information is available in accessible formats. Calls to the Helpline are charged at local rate.

Website: www.drc-gb.org

Telephone: 08457 622 633

Textphone: 08457 622 644

Fax: 08457 778 878

Post: DRC Helpline
               FREEPOST MID02164
               Stratford upon Avon
               CV37 9BR

2 How can discrimination be avoided?

Introduction

2.1 Prevention is better than cure. There are various actions which employers can take in order to avoid discriminating against disabled people. By doing so, employers are not only likely to minimise the incidence of expensive and time-consuming litigation, but will also improve their general performance and the quality of their business operations. This chapter sets out some guidance on ways to help ensure that disabled people are not discriminated against.

Understanding the social dimension of disability

2.2 The concept of discrimination in the Act reflects an understanding that functional limitations arising from disabled people's impairments do not inevitably restrict their ability to participate fully in society. Rather than the limitations of an impairment, it is often environmental factors (such as the structure of a building, or an employer's working practices) which unnecessarily lead to these social restrictions. This principle underpins the duty to make reasonable adjustments described in Chapter 5. Understanding this will assist employers and others to avoid discrimination. It is as important to consider which aspects of employment and occupation create difficulties for a disabled person as it is to understand the particular nature of an individual's disability.

Recognising the diverse nature of disability

2.3 There are around ten million disabled adults in our society. The nature and extent of their disabilities vary widely, as do their requirements for overcoming any difficulties they may face. If employers are to avoid discriminating, they need to understand this, and to be aware of the effects their decisions and actions – and those of their agents and employees – may have on disabled people. The evidence shows that many of the steps that can be taken to avoid discrimination cost little or nothing and are easy to implement.

Avoiding making assumptions

2.4 It is advisable to avoid making assumptions about disabled people. Disabilities will often affect different people in different ways and their needs may be different as well. The following suggestions may help to avoid discrimination:

- Do not assume that because a person does not look disabled, he is not disabled.

- Do not assume that because you do not know of any disabled people working within an organisation there are none.

- Do not assume that most disabled people use wheelchairs.

- Do not assume that people with learning disabilities cannot be valuable employees, or that they can only do low status jobs.

- Do not assume that a person with a mental health problem cannot do a demanding job.

- Do not assume that all blind people read Braille or have guide dogs.

- Do not assume that all deaf people use sign language.

- Do not assume that because a disabled person may have less employment experience (in paid employment) than a non-disabled person, he has less to offer.

Finding out about disabled people's needs

2.5 As explained later in the Code (see paragraphs 7.22 and 8.16 for example), the Act requires employers to think about ways of complying with their legal duties. Listening carefully to disabled people and finding out what they want will help employers to meet their obligations by identifying the best way of meeting disabled people's needs. There is a better chance of reaching the best outcome if discussions are held with disabled people at an early stage.

2.6 Often, discussing with disabled people what is required to meet their needs will reassure an employer that suitable adjustments can be carried out cheaply and with very little inconvenience.

2.7 Evidence shows that in meeting the needs of disabled employees an organisation learns how to meet the needs of disabled customers, and vice versa. By consulting with disabled employees, an organisation can therefore improve the service it provides to its disabled customers and enhance its business.

2.8 There are various ways in which the views of disabled people can be obtained. Many larger employers have established formal structures for seeking and representing the views of disabled people. Small employers can also consult with disabled employees, although the methods may be less formal.

A large employer sets up a network through which disabled employees can discuss their concerns and make recommendations to management, either directly or via a recognised trade union.

A small employer asks a disabled employee if he has any concerns about how a reorganisation of the business will impact upon him.

Seeking expert advice

2.9 It may be possible to avoid discrimination by using personal or in-house knowledge and expertise – particularly if information or views are obtained from the disabled person concerned. However, although the Act does not specifically require anyone to obtain expert advice about meeting the needs of disabled people with regard to employment, in practice it may sometimes be necessary to do so in order to comply with the principal duties set out in the Act. Expert advice might be especially useful if a person is newly disabled or if the effects of a person's disability become more marked. Expert advice about meeting the needs of disabled people may be available from local Jobcentre Plus offices, or from local and national disability organisations.

Planning ahead

2.10 The duties which the Act places on employers are owed to the individual disabled people with whom they have dealings. There is no duty owed to disabled people in general. Nevertheless, it is likely to be cost effective for employers to plan ahead. Considering the needs of a range of disabled people when planning for change (such as when planning a building refurbishment, a new IT system, or the design of a website) is likely to make it easier to implement adjustments for individuals when the need arises.

2.11 It is good practice for employers to have access audits carried out to identify any improvements which can be made to a building to make it more accessible. Access audits should be carried out by suitably qualified people, such as those listed in the National Register of Access Consultants (see Appendix C for details). Websites and intranet sites can also be reviewed to see how accessible they are to disabled people using access software.

> The owner of a small shop is planning a refit of her premises. As part of the refit she asks the designers to comply with British Standard 8300 to ensure that the shop has a good standard of access for a variety of disabled people, whether customers or employees. BS 8300 is a code of practice on the design of buildings and their approaches to meet the needs of disabled people (see Appendix C for details).

> An employer is re-designing its website, which it uses to promote the company as well as to advertise vacancies. The employer ensures that the new design for the website is easy to read for people with a variety of access software; has the website checked for accessibility; and invites disabled readers of the website to let the employer know if they find any part of it inaccessible.

Implementing anti-discriminatory policies and practices

2.12 Employers are more likely to comply with their duties under the Act, and to avoid the risk of legal action being taken against them, if they implement anti-discriminatory policies and practices. These are often referred to as equality policies or diversity policies. Additionally, in the event that legal action is taken, employers may be asked to demonstrate to an employment tribunal that they have effective policies and procedures in place to minimise the risk of discrimination. Although large and small employers are likely to have different kinds of anti-discriminatory policies and practices, it is advisable for all employers to take the following steps:

- Establish a policy which aims to prevent discrimination against disabled people and which is communicated to all employees and agents of the employer.

- Provide disability awareness and equality training to all employees. In addition, train employees and agents so that they understand the employer's policy on disability, their obligations under the Act and the practice of reasonable adjustments. People within the organisation who have responsibility for managing, recruiting or training employees are likely to need more specialist training.

- Inform all employees and agents that conduct which breaches the policy will not be tolerated, and respond quickly and effectively to any such breaches.

- Monitor the implementation and effectiveness of such a policy.

- Address acts of disability discrimination by employees as part of disciplinary rules and procedures.

- Have complaints and grievance procedures which are easy for disabled people to use and which are designed to resolve issues effectively.

- Have clear procedures to prevent and deal with harassment for a reason related to a person's disability.

- Establish a policy in relation to disability-related leave, and monitor the implementation and effectiveness of such a policy.

- Consult with disabled employees about their experiences of working for the organisation.

- Regularly review the effectiveness of reasonable adjustments made for disabled people in accordance with the Act, and act on the findings of those reviews.

- Keep clear records of decisions taken in respect of each of these matters.

When a large company introduces a new disability policy, it might ask an external training company to run training sessions for all staff, or it might ask a human resources manager to deliver training to staff on this policy. The external training company might be one run by disabled people.

A small employer introducing a similar policy asks the managing director to devote a team meeting to explaining the policy to her staff and to discuss why it is important and how it will operate.

A large employer trains all its employees in disability equality, the organisation's disability policy and the Disability Discrimination Act. It also trains all occupational health advisers with whom it works to ensure that they have the necessary expertise about the Act and the organisation's disability policy.

A small employer only uses occupational health advisers who can demonstrate that they have knowledge of the Act.

A large employer issues a questionnaire to employees about the organisation's attitude to disability, inviting suggestions for improvements.

A small employer asks disabled employees to feed back views on the employer's approach to disability issues.

Auditing policies and procedures

2.13 Although there is no duty under Part 2 to anticipate the needs of disabled people in general, it is a good idea for employers to keep all their policies under review, and to consider the needs of disabled people as part of this process. It is advisable for employers to do this in addition to having a specific policy to prevent discrimination. Employers are likely to have policies about matters such as:

- flexible working arrangements

- appraisal and performance-related pay systems

- sickness absence

- redundancy selection criteria

- emergency evacuation procedures

- procurement of equipment, IT systems, software and websites

- information provision

- employee training and development

- employee assistance schemes offering financial or emotional support.

An organisation has a policy to ensure that all employees are kept informed about the organisation's activities through an intranet site. The policy says that the intranet site should be accessible to all employees, including those who use access software (such as synthetic speech output) because of their disabilities.

An employer has a policy of having annual appraisal interviews for all employees. The policy says that during the interviews, disabled employees should be asked whether they need any (further) reasonable adjustments. This could equally apply to a large or small employer.

An employer introduces a system for performance-related pay. It takes advice on performance-related pay systems from an employers' organisation, to ensure that the system it introduces is an effective tool for improving performance and is fair to all employees. It also ensures that every year the system is monitored to ensure that disabled people do not, on average, get lower awards.

A redundancy policy that has sickness absence as a selection criterion is amended to exclude disability-related absence. The sickness absence policy is also changed so that disability-related sickness is recorded separately.

A new procurement policy requires a number of factors to be taken into account in procuring equipment and IT systems. These factors include cost and energy efficiency. It is good practice for such factors to include accessibility for disabled people as well.

Emergency evacuation policies and procedures are reviewed to ensure that there are individual evacuation plans for any disabled people who need them.

Monitoring

2.14 Monitoring of employees is an important way of determining whether anti-discrimination measures taken by an organisation are effective, and ensuring that disability equality is a reality within that organisation. Information must be gathered sensitively, with appropriately worded questions, and confidentiality must be ensured. Knowing the proportion of disabled people at various levels of the organisation, and at various stages in relation to the recruitment process, can help an organisation determine where practices and policies need to be improved. The extent to which formal monitoring can be carried out will depend on the size of the organisation.

2.15 Monitoring will be more effective if employees (or job applicants) feel comfortable about disclosing information about their disabilities. This is more likely to be the case if the employer explains the purpose of the monitoring and if employees or job applicants believe that the employer genuinely values disabled employees and is using the information gathered to create positive change.

Through monitoring of candidates at the recruitment stage an employer becomes aware that, although several disabled people applied for a post, none was short-listed for interview. It uses this information to review the essential requirements for the post.

2.16 Some organisations, especially large ones, choose to monitor by broad type of disability to understand the barriers faced by people with different types of impairment.

A large employer notices through monitoring that the organisation has been successful at retaining most groups of disabled people, but not people with mental health problems. It acts on this information by contacting a specialist organisation for advice about good practice in retaining people with mental health problems.

Ensuring good practice in recruitment

Attracting disabled applicants

2.17 An organisation which recognises that suitably qualified disabled people have not applied to work for it may want to make contact with local employment services, including Jobcentre Plus and specialist disability employment services, to encourage disabled people to apply. It is normally lawful for an employer to advertise a vacancy as open only to disabled people (see paragraph 7.5).

By monitoring the recruitment process a small employer notices that very few disabled people apply to work for it. In the light of this information, it decides to notify local disability employment projects of its vacancies.

A retailer has a number of vacancies to fill. It contacts Jobcentre Plus and arranges an open morning for local disabled people to find out more about working for this employer.

Through its monitoring process, a medium-sized employer becomes aware of the fact that disabled people are under-represented in its workforce. It is looking for people to fill 3 work experience placements and decides to offer these placements to disabled people only.

A museum wants to understand the needs of its disabled visitors better. It decides to change its person specifications for posts in the visitor services department to include a requirement to have knowledge of disability access issues. It notifies local employment services for disabled people of these posts.

2.18 It is good practice to consider carefully what information should be included in advertisements and where they should be placed.

An advertisement which specifies that flexible working is available may encourage more disabled applicants to apply.

An advertisement that appears in the disability press and a local talking newspaper may encourage disabled applicants to apply.

Promoting a positive image

2.19 It is good practice for an employer to consider its image to ensure that it gives an impression of itself as an organisation that is aware of the needs of disabled people and is striving to create a more diverse workforce.

A large employer ensures that its recruitment brochure includes images of disabled employees, and contains information about its disability policy.

A small employer advertises in a local newspaper. The advertisement states that disabled people are encouraged to apply.

Use of the Disability Symbol

2.20 The Disability Symbol is a recognition given to employers by Jobcentre Plus. An employer displaying the Disability Symbol must commit itself to a number of measures concerning the recruitment, development and retention of disabled people, including offering a guaranteed interview to any disabled person who meets the essential requirements of the job. It is important that employers make clear what those essential requirements are. For more information about the Disability Symbol see Appendix C.

Resolving disputes

2.21 Having policies and practices to combat discrimination, together with regular consultation with employees, is likely to minimise disputes about disability discrimination. But when such disputes do occur, it is in the interests of employers to attempt wherever possible to resolve them as they arise. Grievance procedures can provide an open and fair way for employees to make their concerns known, and can enable grievances to be resolved quickly before they become major problems. Use of the procedures may highlight areas in which the duty to make reasonable adjustments has not been observed, and can prevent misunderstandings leading to complaints to tribunals. It is important to ensure that grievance procedures are accessible to disabled people.

2.22 In certain circumstances, employers and employees are required by law to comply with internal dispute resolution procedures before making a complaint to a tribunal. Chapter 13 contains further information about grievance procedures and about resolving disputes under the Act. Whether or not an attempt at internal resolution of a dispute is made as a result of a legal requirement, it should be carried out in a non-discriminatory way to comply with the Act.

2

3 The Act's provisions on employment and occupation — an overview

Introduction

3.1 This chapter gives an overview of the provisions of the Act relating to employment and occupation. It explains who has rights and duties under those provisions and outlines what is made unlawful by them. Later chapters explain the provisions in greater detail.

Who has rights under the Act?

Disabled people

3.2 The Act gives protection from discrimination to a 'disabled' person within the meaning of the Act. A disabled person is someone who has a physical or mental impairment which has an effect on his or her ability to carry out normal day-to-day activities. That effect must be:

ss 1 & 2
Sch 1 & 2

- substantial (that is, more than minor or trivial), and

- adverse, and

- long term (that is, it has lasted or is likely to last for at least a year or for the rest of the life of the person affected).

3.3 Physical or mental impairment includes sensory impairment. Hidden impairments are also covered (for example, mental illness or mental health problems, learning disabilities, dyslexia, diabetes and epilepsy).

3.4 In considering its duties under the Act, an employer should not use any definition of 'disabled person' which is narrower than that in the Act. An employer who is requested to make a disability-related adjustment may ask the person requesting it for evidence that the impairment is one which meets the definition of disability in the Act. It may be appropriate to do so where the disability is not obvious. However, employers should not ask for more information about the impairment than is necessary for this purpose. Nor should they ask for evidence of disability where it ought to be obvious that the Act will apply.

> A woman with ME (chronic fatigue syndrome) asks for time off to attend regular hospital appointments. The employer could legitimately ask to see a letter from the doctor or an appointment card. However, the employer then asks her questions about the likely progress of the illness so that he can bear this in mind when thinking about restructuring the department. This is likely to be unlawful.

People who have had a disability in the past

3.5 People who have had a disability within the meaning of the Act in the past are protected from discrimination even if they no longer have the disability.

> A job applicant discloses on her application form that while at university from 1992 to 1993 she had long-term clinical depression after her father died. It would be discrimination to refuse to interview or recruit her because she has had a disability in the past. The fact that the disability preceded the Disability Discrimination Act 1995 is irrelevant.

3.6 For a fuller understanding of the concept of disability under the Act, reference should be made to Appendix B. A government publication, **Guidance on matters to be taken into account in determining questions relating to the definition of disability,** provides additional help in understanding the concept of disability and in identifying who is a disabled person. Where relevant, the Guidance must be taken into account in any legal proceedings.

People who have been victimised

3.7 The Act also gives rights to people who have been victimised, whether or not they have a disability or have had one in the past. (see paragraphs 4.33 to 4.36).

Who has obligations under the Act?

Employers

3.8 Later chapters explain in detail the duties which the Act imposes upon employers. The Act defines 'employment' as employment under a contract of service or of apprenticeship or a contract personally to do any work. Anyone who works under a contract falling within this definition is an employee, whether or not, for example, he works full-time.

s 68(1)

3.9 Members of the Armed Forces are excluded from protection under the Act's provisions on employment and occupation. Otherwise, those provisions now apply to all employers in respect of people they employ wholly or partly at an establishment in Great Britain. Protection under the Act extends to employment wholly outside Great Britain, provided that the employment has a sufficiently close connection with Great Britain –

s 64(7)

s 4(6)

s 68(2) - (2D)

and the Act sets out the circumstances in which this will be the case. Certain employment on board ships, hovercraft and aircraft is also covered.

3.10 A person who is recruiting an employee has duties under the Act even if he is not yet an employer (because the new recruit will be his first employee).

People or bodies concerned with certain occupations

3.11 The Act's definition of employment is wide enough to include people who are self-employed but who agree to perform work personally. The provisions of Part 2 also extend to the following occupations which do not fall within the definition of employment:

- contract workers

- office holders

- police officers

- partners in firms

- barristers and advocates

- people undertaking practical work experience for a limited period for the purposes of vocational training.

Many of the principles which apply to employers under Part 2 are equally applicable in respect of these occupations. Further details about the application of the Act's provisions on employment and occupation in this regard are set out in Chapter 9.

Others to whom Part 2 applies

3.12 In addition, the Act's provisions on employment and occupation may also impose obligations upon the following people and organisations:

- trustees and managers of occupational pension schemes (see Chapter 10)

- insurers who provide group insurance services for an employer's employees (see Chapter 10)

- landlords of premises occupied by an employer or other person to whom Part 2 applies (see Chapter 12)

- employees and agents of a person to whom Part 2 applies

- Ministers of the Crown, government departments and agencies.

Providers of employment services

3.13 The Act also contains provisions to prevent discrimination by people or organisations who provide employment services – such as employment agencies and careers guidance services (see Chapter 11).

s 21A

Trade organisations and qualifications bodies

3.14 Finally, Part 2 makes special provision in respect of discrimination against disabled people by trade organisations and qualifications bodies. The nature and effect of the provisions in question is explained in a separate code of practice issued by the DRC (see Appendix C for details).

ss 13 - 14B

3

What does the Act say about discrimination in relation to employment and occupation?

3.15 The Act makes it unlawful for an employer to **discriminate** against a disabled person in relation to the recruitment or retention of staff.

3.16 However, the Act does not prohibit an employer from appointing the best person for the job. Nor does it prevent employers from treating disabled people more favourably than those who are not disabled.

Forms of discrimination

3.17 The four forms of discrimination which are unlawful under Part 2 are:

- direct discrimination (the meaning of which is explained at paragraphs 4.5 to 4.23)

- failure to comply with a duty to make reasonable adjustments (explained in Chapter 5)

- 'disability-related discrimination' (see paragraphs 4.27 to 4.32), and

- victimisation of a person (whether or not he is disabled) – what the Act says about victimisation is explained at paragraphs 4.33 to 4.36.

Aspects of employment in respect of which discrimination is unlawful

s 4(1) 3.18 In relation to recruitment, the Act says that it is unlawful for an employer to discriminate against a disabled person:

- in the arrangements made for determining who should be offered employment

- in the terms on which the disabled person is offered employment, or

- by refusing to offer, or deliberately not offering, the disabled person employment.

What this means in practice is explained in Chapter 7.

3.19 In relation to the retention of staff, the Act says that it is unlawful for an employer to discriminate against a disabled person whom it employs:

s 4(2)

- in the terms of employment which it affords him

- in the opportunities which it affords him for promotion, a transfer, training or receiving any other benefit

- by refusing to afford him, or deliberately not affording him, any such opportunity, or

- by dismissing him, or subjecting him to any other detriment.

What this means in practice is explained in Chapter 8.

3.20 The Act also makes it unlawful for an employer to discriminate against a disabled person after that person's employment has come to an end (see paragraph 8.28).

s 16A(3)

What else is unlawful under the Act's provisions on employment and occupation?

Harassment

3.21 In addition to what it says about discrimination, Part 2 makes it unlawful, in relation to the recruitment or retention of staff, for an employer to subject a disabled person to **harassment** for a

s 3B

reason which relates to his disability. What the Act says about harassment is explained in more detail at paragraphs 4.38 and 4.39.

s 16C

s 17B(1)

3.22 It is also unlawful for a person who has authority or influence over another to instruct him, or put pressure on him, to act unlawfully under the provisions of Part 2 (or, insofar as they relate to employment services, Part 3). This covers pressure to discriminate, whether applied directly to the person concerned, or indirectly but in a way in which he is likely to hear of it. However, the Act does not give individual disabled people the right to take legal action in respect of unlawful instructions or pressure to discriminate. Such action may only be taken by the DRC (see paragraphs 13.28 to 13.30).

Who is liable for unlawful acts?

Responsibility for the acts of others

s 58

3.23 Employers who act through agents (such as occupational health advisers or recruitment agencies) are liable for the actions of their agents done with the employer's express or implied authority. The Act also says that employers are responsible for the actions of their employees in the course of their employment. However, in legal proceedings against an employer based on the actions of an employee, it is a defence that the employer took 'such steps as were reasonably practicable' to prevent such actions. It is not a defence for the employer simply to show that the action took place without its knowledge or approval. Chapter 2 gives guidance on the steps which it might be appropriate to take for this purpose.

A shopkeeper goes abroad for 3 months and leaves his son in charge of the shop. While he is away his son picks on a shop assistant with a learning disability, by constantly criticising her work unfairly. The shop assistant leaves her job as a result of this bullying. The shopkeeper is responsible for the actions of his son.

Aiding an unlawful act

3.24   A person who knowingly helps another to do something made unlawful by the Act will be treated as having done the same kind of unlawful act. This means that, where an employer is liable for an unlawful act of its employee or agent, that employee or agent will be liable for aiding the unlawful act of the employer.

s 57

A recruitment consultant engaged by an engineering company refuses to consider a disabled applicant for a vacancy, because the company has told the consultant that it does not want the post filled by someone who is 'handicapped'. Under the Act the consultant could be liable for aiding the company to discriminate, in addition to the company's own liability for its unlawful act.

3.25   Where an employee discriminates against or harasses a disabled employee, it is the employer who will be liable for that unlawful act – unless it can show that it took such steps as were reasonable to prevent the unlawful act in question. But the employee who committed the discrimination or harassment will be liable for aiding the unlawful act – and this will be the case even if the employer is able to show that it took reasonable steps to prevent the act.

An employer has policies relating to harassment and disability. It ensures that all employees are aware of the policies and of the fact that harassment of disabled employees is subject to disciplinary action. It also ensures that managers receive training in applying the policies. A woman with a learning disability is humiliated by a colleague and disciplinary action is taken against the colleague. In these circumstances the colleague would be liable for aiding the unlawful act of the employer (the harassment) even though the employer would itself avoid liability because it had taken reasonably practicable steps to prevent the unlawful act.

Enforcing rights under Part 2

s 17A

3.26 Enforcement of rights under Part 2 takes place in the employment tribunals. Enforcement of rights under the Act in relation to the provision of employment services also takes place in the employment tribunals. More information about enforcement is given in Chapter 13.

Introduction

4.1 As noted at paragraph 3.17, the forms of discrimination which the Act makes unlawful in relation to employment are:

- direct discrimination

- failure to comply with a duty to make reasonable adjustments

- disability-related discrimination, and

- victimisation.

4.2 This chapter describes these four forms of discrimination in more detail, and explains the differences between them. It explores, in particular, the distinction between direct discrimination and disability-related discrimination (see paragraphs 4.28 to 4.31). These two forms of discrimination both depend on the way in which the employer treats the disabled person concerned – both require the disabled person to have been treated less favourably than other people are (or would be) treated. However, whether such treatment amounts to one of these forms of discrimination or the other (and, indeed, whether the treatment is unlawful in the first place) depends on the circumstances in which it arose.

4.3 The chapter examines the four forms of discrimination in the order in which they are listed in paragraph 4.1. This is because less favourable treatment which does not amount to direct discrimination can sometimes be justified. (In contrast, neither direct discrimination nor a failure to comply with a duty to make a reasonable adjustment is justifiable. Victimisation cannot be justified either.) In deciding whether the treatment is justified, and therefore whether there has been disability-related discrimination, the Act requires the question of reasonable adjustments to be taken into account (see paragraphs 6.4 and 6.5 where this is explained in more detail). Consequently, although the chapter describes direct discrimination first, it touches on the subject of reasonable adjustments before moving on to disability-related discrimination.

4.4 This chapter also explains what the Act means by 'harassment'. The concepts of discrimination and harassment are relevant not only in relation to employment but also to the application of Part 2 in other situations – for example, in relation to the occupations mentioned in Chapter 9. The provisions about discrimination and harassment in Part 2 are also relevant to what the Act says about employment services in Part 3. This is described in Chapter 11.

What does the Act mean by 'direct discrimination'?

What does the Act say?

s 3A(5) 4.5 The Act says that an employer's treatment of a disabled person amounts to direct discrimination if:

- it is on the ground of his disability

- the treatment is less favourable than the way in which a person not having that particular disability is (or would be) treated, and

- the relevant circumstances, including the abilities, of the person with whom the comparison is made are the same as, or not materially different from, those of the disabled person.

4.6 It follows that direct discrimination depends on an employer's treatment of a disabled person being on the ground of his disability. It also depends on a comparison of that treatment with the way in which the employer treats (or would treat) an appropriate comparator. If, on the ground of his disability, the disabled person is treated less favourably than the comparator is (or would be) treated, the treatment amounts to direct discrimination.

When is direct discrimination likely to occur?

4.7 Treatment of a disabled person is 'on the ground of' his disability if it is caused by the fact that he is disabled or has the disability in question. In general, this means that treatment is on the ground of disability if a disabled person would not have received it but for his disability. However, disability does not have to be the only (or even the main) cause of the treatment complained of – provided that it is an effective cause, determined objectively from all the circumstances.

4.8 Consequently, if the less favourable treatment occurs because of the employer's generalised, or stereotypical, assumptions about the disability or its effects, it is likely to be direct discrimination. This is because an employer would not normally make such assumptions about a non-disabled person, but would instead consider his individual abilities.

4

A blind woman is not short-listed for a job involving computers because the employer wrongly assumes that blind people cannot use them. The employer makes no attempt to look at the individual circumstances. The employer has treated the woman less favourably than other people by not short-listing her for the job. The treatment was on the ground of the woman's disability (because assumptions would not have been made about a non-disabled person).

4.9 In addition, less favourable treatment which is disability-specific, or which arises out of prejudice about disability (or about a particular type of disability), is also likely to amount to direct discrimination.

An employer seeking a shop assistant turns down a disabled applicant with a severe facial disfigurement solely on the ground that other employees would be uncomfortable working alongside him. This would amount to direct discrimination and would be unlawful.

A disabled woman who uses a wheelchair applies for a job. She can do the job just as well as any other applicant, but the employer wrongly assumes that the wheelchair will cause an obstruction in the office. He therefore gives the job to a person who is no more suitable for the job but who is not a wheelchair-user. This would amount to direct discrimination and would be unlawful.

4.10 In some cases, an apparently neutral reason for less favourable treatment of a disabled person may, on investigation, turn out to be a pretext for direct discrimination.

4.11 Direct discrimination will often occur where the employer is aware that the disabled person has a disability, and this is the reason for the employer's treatment of him. Direct discrimination need not be conscious – people may hold prejudices that they do not admit, even to themselves. Thus, a person may behave in a discriminatory way while believing that he would never do so. Moreover, direct discrimination may sometimes occur even though the employer is unaware of a person's disability.

An employer advertises a promotion internally to its workforce. The job description states that people with a history of mental illness would not be suitable for the post. An employee who would otherwise be eligible for the promotion has a history of schizophrenia, but the employer is unaware of this. The employee would, nevertheless, have a good claim for unlawful direct discrimination in relation to the promotion opportunities afforded to him by his employer. The act of direct discrimination in this case is the blanket ban on anyone who has had a mental illness, effectively rejecting whole categories of people with no consideration of their individual abilities.

4.12 In situations such as those described in the above examples, it will often be readily apparent that the disabled person concerned has been treated less favourably on the ground of his disability. In other cases, however, this may be less obvious. Whether or not the basis for the treatment in question appears to be clear, a useful way of telling whether or not it is discriminatory, (and of establishing what kind of discrimination it is), is to focus on the person with whom the disabled person should be compared. That person may be real or hypothetical (see paragraph 4.18).

Identifying comparators in respect of direct discrimination

4.13 In determining whether a disabled person has been treated less favourably in the context of direct discrimination, his treatment must be compared with that of an appropriate comparator. This must be someone who does not have the same disability. It could be a non-disabled person or a person with other disabilities.

A person who becomes disabled takes six months' sick leave because of his disability, and is dismissed by his employer. A non-disabled fellow employee also takes six months' sick leave (because he has broken his leg) but is not dismissed. The difference in treatment is attributable to the employer's unwillingness to employ disabled staff and the treatment is therefore on the ground of disability. The non-disabled employee is an appropriate comparator in the context of direct discrimination because his relevant circumstances are the same as those of the disabled person. It is the fact of having taken six months' sick leave which is relevant in these circumstances. As the disabled person has been treated less favourably than the comparator, this is direct discrimination.

4.14 It follows that, in the great majority of cases, some difference will exist between the circumstances (including the abilities) of the comparator and those of the disabled person – there is no need to find a comparator whose circumstances are the same as those of the disabled person in every respect. What matters is that the comparator's **relevant** circumstances (including his abilities) must be the same as, or not materially different from, those of the disabled person.

In the previous example, the position would be different if it were the employer's policy to dismiss any member of staff who has been off sick for six months, and that policy were applied equally to disabled and non-disabled staff. In this case there would be no direct discrimination because the disabled person would not have been treated less favourably than the comparator – both would have been dismissed. Nevertheless, there may be a claim for failure to make reasonable adjustments to the policy, for example by allowing disability leave (see paragraph 4.25). In addition, the employer's policy may give rise to a claim for disability-related discrimination (see paragraph 4.27).

4.15 Once an appropriate comparator is identified, it is clear that the situation described in the example at paragraph 4.8 amounts to direct discrimination:

In the example about the blind woman who is not short-listed for a job involving computers, there is direct discrimination because the woman was treated less favourably on the ground of her disability than an appropriate comparator (that is, a person who is not blind but who has the same abilities to do the job as the blind applicant): such a person would not have been rejected out of hand without consideration of her individual abilities.

4.16 The examples of direct discrimination in paragraph 4.9 also become clearer when the appropriate comparator is identified in each case:

In the example about the disabled person with a severe facial disfigurement who applies to be a shop assistant, there is direct discrimination because the man was treated less favourably on the ground of his disability than an appropriate comparator (that is, a person who does not have such a disfigurement but who does have the same abilities to do the job): such a person would not have been rejected in the same way.

In the example about the disabled woman who is not offered a job because she uses a wheelchair, there is direct discrimination because the woman was treated less favourably on the ground of her disability than an appropriate comparator (that is, a person who does not use a wheelchair but who does have the same abilities to do the job): such a person would not have been rejected in the same way.

4.17 The comparator used in relation to direct discrimination under the Act is the same as it is for other types of direct discrimination – such as direct sex discrimination. It is, however, made explicit in the Act that the comparator must have the same relevant abilities as the disabled person.

4.18 It may not be possible to identify an actual comparator whose relevant circumstances are the same as (or not materially different from) those of the disabled person in question. In such cases a hypothetical comparator may be used. Evidence which helps to establish how a hypothetical comparator would have been treated is likely to include details of how other people (not satisfying the statutory comparison test) were treated in circumstances which were broadly similar.

A disabled person works in a restaurant. She makes a mistake on the till and this results in a small financial loss to her employer. She is dismissed because of this. The situation has not arisen before, and so there is no actual comparator. Nevertheless, six months earlier a non-disabled fellow employee was disciplined for taking home items of food without permission and received a written warning. The treatment of that person might be used as evidence that a hypothetical non-disabled member of staff who makes an error on the till would not have been dismissed for that reason.

4.19 It should be noted that the type of comparator described in the preceding paragraphs is only relevant to disability discrimination when assessing whether there has been **direct** discrimination. A different comparison falls to be made when assessing whether there has been a failure to comply with a duty to make reasonable adjustments (see paragraphs 5.3 and 5.4) or when considering disability-related discrimination (see paragraph 4.30).

Focusing on relevant circumstances

4.20 As stated in paragraph 4.14, direct discrimination only occurs where the **relevant** circumstances of the comparator, including his abilities, are the same as, or not materially different from, those of the disabled person himself. It is therefore important to focus on those circumstances which are, in fact, relevant to the matter to which the less favourable treatment relates. Although, in some cases, the effects of the disability may be relevant, the fact of the disability itself is not a relevant circumstance for these purposes. This is because the comparison must be with a person **not** having that particular disability.

A disabled person with arthritis who can type at 30 words per minute (wpm) applies for an administrative job which includes typing, but is rejected on the ground that her typing speed is too slow. The correct comparator in a claim for direct discrimination would be a person not having arthritis who also has a typing speed of 30 wpm (with the same accuracy rate).

A disabled person with a severe visual impairment applies for a job as a bus driver and is refused the job because he fails to meet the minimum level of visual acuity which is essential to the safe performance of the job. The correct comparator is a person not having that particular disability (for example, a person who merely has poorer than average eyesight) also failing to meet that minimum standard.

A disabled person with schizophrenia applies for a job as an administrative assistant with his local authority, and declares his history of mental illness. The local authority refuses him employment, relying on a negative medical report from the authority's occupational health adviser which is based on assumptions about the effects of schizophrenia, without adequate consideration of the individual's abilities and the impact of the impairment in his particular case. This is likely to amount to direct discrimination and to be unlawful. The comparator here is a person who does not have schizophrenia, but who has the same abilities to do the job (including relevant qualifications and experience) as the disabled applicant: such a person would not have been rejected without adequate consideration of his individual abilities.

4.21 If (as in the above examples) a disabled person alleges that he has been refused the offer of a job on the ground of his disability, it is only appropriate to compare those of his circumstances which are relevant to his ability to do the job. It is not appropriate to compare other circumstances which are not relevant to this issue. The need to focus on relevant circumstances applies not only to recruitment cases of this kind, but also to any other situation where direct discrimination may have occurred.

A disabled man with arthritis applies for an administrative job which includes typing, but is rejected in favour of a non-disabled candidate. Because of his arthritis, the man has a slow typing speed and has difficulty walking. The job is entirely desk-based, and does not require the person doing it to be able to walk further than a few metres within the office. The comparator in a claim of direct discrimination would be a non-disabled applicant with the same slow typing speed (and with the same abilities to do the job – e.g., the same typing accuracy rate, and the same knowledge of word-processing packages) – but it would not be necessary for the comparator to have mobility problems (because the ability to walk further than a few metres is not relevant to the candidates' ability to do the job).

4

4.22 In making the comparison in respect of a claim of direct discrimination, the disabled person's abilities must be considered **as they in fact are**. In some cases, there will be particular reasonable adjustments which an employer was required by the Act to make, but in fact failed to make. It may be that those adjustments would have had an effect on the disabled person's abilities to do the job. But in making the comparison, the disabled person's abilities should be considered as they **in fact** were, and not as they would or might have been had those adjustments been made. On the other hand, if adjustments have **in fact** been made which have had the effect of enhancing the disabled person's abilities, then it is those enhanced abilities which should be considered. The disabled person's abilities are being considered as they in fact are (and not as they might have been if the adjustments had not been made).

A disabled person who applies for an administrative job which includes typing is not allowed to use her own adapted keyboard (even though it would have been reasonable for the employer to allow this) and types a test document at 30 wpm. Her speed with the adapted keyboard would have been 50 wpm. A non-disabled candidate is given the job because her typing speed on the test was 45 wpm with the same accuracy rate. This is not direct discrimination, as the comparator is a non-disabled person typing at 30 wpm. (But the disabled person would be likely to have good claims in respect of two other forms of discrimination - failure to make reasonable adjustments and disability-related discrimination - see paragraph 4.37.)

> A disabled person with arthritis who applies for a similar job is allowed to use an adapted keyboard and types a test document at 50 wpm. A non-disabled candidate types at 30 wpm with the same accuracy rate. However, the disabled candidate is rejected because of prejudice and the other candidate is offered the job instead. This is direct discrimination, as the comparator would be a person not having arthritis who could type at 50 wpm.

Can direct discrimination be justified?

4.23 Treatment of a disabled person which amounts to direct discrimination under the Act's provisions on employment and occupation is unlawful. It can never be justified.

s 3A(4)

Failure to make reasonable adjustments – relationship to discrimination

4.24 For the reason given in paragraph 4.3, it may be necessary to consider whether an employer has failed to comply with a duty to make a reasonable adjustment in order to determine whether disability-related discrimination has occurred.

4.25 Irrespective of its relevance to disability-related discrimination, however, a failure to comply with a duty to make a reasonable adjustment in respect of a disabled person amounts to discrimination in its own right. Such a failure is therefore unlawful. Chapter 5 explains the circumstances in which an employer has such a duty, and gives guidance as to what employers need to do when the duty arises.

s 3A(2)

4.26 As with direct discrimination, the Act does not permit an employer to justify a failure to comply with a duty to make a reasonable adjustment (see paragraphs 5.43 and 5.44).

What is disability-related discrimination?

What does the Act say?

s 3A(1)

4.27 The Act says that an employer's treatment of a disabled person amounts to discrimination if:

- it is for a reason related to his disability

- the treatment is less favourable than the way in which the employer treats (or would treat) others to whom that reason does not (or would not) apply, and

- the employer cannot show that the treatment is justified.

4.28 Although the Act itself does not use the term 'disability-related discrimination', this expression is used in the Code when referring to treatment of a disabled person which:

- is unlawful because each of the conditions listed in paragraph 4.27 is satisfied, but

- does not amount to direct discrimination under the Act.

4.29 In general, direct discrimination occurs when the reason for the less favourable treatment in question is the disability, while disability-related discrimination occurs when the reason relates to the disability but is not the disability itself. The expression 'disability-related discrimination' therefore distinguishes less favourable treatment which amounts to direct discrimination from a wider class of less favourable treatment which, although not amounting to direct discrimination, is nevertheless unlawful.

4

4.30 In determining whether disability-related discrimination has occurred, the employer's treatment of the disabled person must be compared with that of a person **to whom the disability-related reason does not apply**. This contrasts with direct discrimination, which requires a comparison to be made with a person without the disability in question but whose relevant circumstances are the same. The comparator may be non-disabled or disabled – but the key point is that the disability-related reason for the less favourable treatment must not apply to him.

> A disabled man is dismissed for taking six months' sick leave which is disability-related. The employer's policy, which has been applied equally to all staff (whether disabled or not) is to dismiss all employees who have taken this amount of sick leave. The disability-related reason for the less favourable treatment of the disabled person is the fact of having taken six months' sick leave, and the correct comparator is a person to whom that reason does not apply – that is, someone who has not taken six months' sick leave. Consequently, unless the employer can show that the treatment is justified, it will amount to disability-related discrimination because the comparator would not have been dismissed. However, the reason for the treatment is not the disability itself (it is only a matter related thereto, namely the amount of sick leave taken). So there is no direct discrimination.

A disabled woman is refused an administrative job because she cannot type. She cannot type because she has arthritis. A non-disabled person who was unable to type would also have been turned down. The disability-related reason for the less favourable treatment is the woman's inability to type, and the correct comparator is a person to whom that reason does not apply – that is, someone who can type. Such a person would not have been refused the job. Nevertheless, the disabled woman has been treated less favourably for a disability-related reason and this will be unlawful unless it can be justified. There is no direct discrimination, however, because the comparator for **direct** discrimination is a person who does not have arthritis, but who is also unable to type.

4.31 The relationship between a disabled person's disability and the employer's treatment of him must be judged objectively. The reason for any less favourable treatment may well relate to the disability even if the employer does not have knowledge of the disability as such, or of whether its salient features are such that it meets the definition of disability in the Act. Less favourable treatment which is not itself direct discrimination will still be unlawful (subject to justification) if, in fact, the reason for it relates to the person's disability.

A woman takes three periods of sickness absence in a two month period because of her disability, which is multiple sclerosis (MS). Her employer is unaware that she has MS and dismisses her, in the same way that it would dismiss any employee for a similar attendance record. Nevertheless, this is less favourable treatment for a disability-related reason (namely, the woman's record of sickness absence) and would be unlawful unless it can be justified.

4.32 The circumstances in which justification may be possible are explained in Chapter 6. However, it is worth noting that the possibility of justifying potential discrimination only arises at all when the form of discrimination being considered is disability-related discrimination, rather than direct discrimination or failure to make reasonable adjustments.

What does the Act say about victimisation?

4.33 Victimisation is a special form of discrimination which is made unlawful by the Act. It is unlawful for one person to treat another ('the victim') less favourably than he treats or would treat other people in the same circumstances because the victim has:

s 55(1) & (2)

- brought, or given evidence or information in connection with, proceedings under the Act (whether or not proceedings are later withdrawn)

- done anything else under or by reference to the Act, or

- alleged someone has contravened the Act (whether or not the allegation is later dropped),

or because the person believes or suspects that the victim has done or intends to do any of these things.

A disabled employee complains of discrimination, having been refused promotion at work. A colleague gives evidence at the tribunal hearing on his behalf. The employer makes the disabled person's colleague redundant because of this. This amounts to victimisation. It would also be unlawful to subject a colleague to any detriment where he attends the tribunal not to give evidence but purely to offer support to the claimant – because this would be something which is done by reference to the Act.

s 55(4)

4.34 It is not victimisation to treat a person less favourably because that person has made an allegation which was false and not made in good faith.

4.35 However, the fact that a person has given evidence on behalf of an applicant in a claim which was unsuccessful does not, of itself, prove that his evidence was false or that it was not given in good faith.

s 55(5)

4.36 Unlike the other forms of discrimination which are made unlawful by the Act, victimisation may be claimed by people who are not disabled as well as by those who are.

How do the different forms of discrimination compare in practice?

4.37 The way in which the different forms of discrimination which are unlawful under the Act's provisions on employment and occupation may operate in practice can be demonstrated by the following series of examples.

A woman with arthritis applies for a secretarial job in a local business. There is a question on the application form about disability, and she indicates that she has arthritis but that it does not affect her typing. The employer rejects her application because it nevertheless wrongly assumes that she will not be able to carry out the job due to her arthritis. This is direct discrimination.

In the situation described above, the woman instead declares on the application form that her arthritis does affect her ability to type. She is called for an interview and is told that a typing test forms part of the selection process. She tells the employer that she will need to use an adapted keyboard in order to take the test, but this is not provided on the day of the interview, and the woman fails the test as a result. As a consequence of failing the test, she is turned down for the job. This is not direct discrimination, as the reason for the employer's rejection of the woman was not her disability, but was the fact that she failed the typing test.

However, in such circumstances the employer has a duty to make reasonable adjustments to its selection arrangements. Depending on the circumstances, it may be a reasonable adjustment for the employer to provide the adapted keyboard or allow the woman to use her own keyboard in order that she is not placed at a substantial disadvantage by the test. If this is the case, then the employer will be unlawfully discriminating against her by failing to make the adjustment.

Although there is no direct discrimination, the employer has still treated the woman less favourably for a reason relating to her disability (namely the fact that she failed the typing test). This will be disability-related discrimination unless the employer can show that it is justified – and the employer will be unable to show this if it would have been reasonable for it to provide her with an adapted keyboard or allow her to use her own in order to take the typing test.

4

Because of the way in which she has been treated, the disabled woman makes a claim against the employer under Part 2 of the Act. Some time later, however, the same employer advertises a further secretarial vacancy. The woman applies again, but the employer rejects her application because she has previously made a claim under the Act. This is victimisation.

What does the Act say about harassment?

s 3B(1)

4.38 The Act says that harassment occurs where, for a reason which relates to a person's disability, another person engages in unwanted conduct which has the purpose or effect of:

- violating the disabled person's dignity, or

- creating an intimidating, hostile, degrading, humiliating or offensive environment for him.

4.39 If the conduct in question was engaged in with the intention that it should have either of these effects, then it amounts to harassment irrespective of its actual effect on the disabled person. In the absence of such intention, however, the conduct will only amount to harassment if it should reasonably be considered as having either of these effects. Regard must be had to all the circumstances in order to determine whether this is the case. Those circumstances include, in particular, the perception of the disabled person.

s 3B(2)

A man with a learning disability is often called 'stupid' and 'slow' by a colleague at work. This is harassment, whether or not the disabled man was present when these comments were made, because they were said with the intention of humiliating him.

A man with a stammer feels he is being harassed because his manager makes constant jokes about people with speech impairments. He asks his manager to stop doing this, but the manager says he is being 'oversensitive' as he habitually makes jokes in the office about many different sorts of people. This is likely to amount to harassment because making remarks of this kind should reasonably be considered as having either of the effects mentioned above.

An employee with HIV uses a colleague's mug. The colleague then makes a point of being seen washing the mug with bleach, which is not something she would do if anyone else used her mug. She also makes offensive comments about having her mug used by someone with HIV. This is likely to amount to harassment.

An employee circulates by email a joke about people with autism. A colleague with autism receives the email and finds the joke offensive. This is likely to amount to harassment.

A woman with depression considers that she is being harassed by her manager who constantly asks her if she is feeling all right, despite the fact that she has asked him not to do so in front of the rest of the team. This could amount to harassment.

What does the Act say about statutory obligations?

s 59

4.40 Nothing is made unlawful by the Act if it is required by an express statutory obligation. However, it is only in cases where a statutory obligation is specific in its requirements, leaving an employer with no choice other than to act in a particular way, that the provisions of the Act may be overridden. The provision in section 59 of the Act is thus of narrow application, and it is likely to permit disability discrimination only in rare circumstances.

What evidence is needed to prove that discrimination or harassment has occurred?

4.41 As stated in paragraph 3.26, enforcement of rights under the Act's provisions on employment and occupation takes place in the employment tribunals. A person who brings a claim for unlawful discrimination or harassment must show that discrimination has occurred. He must prove this on the balance of probabilities in order to succeed with a claim in an employment tribunal.

s 17A(1C)

4.42 However, the Act says that, when such a claim is heard by an employment tribunal, the tribunal must uphold the claim if:

- the claimant proves facts from which the tribunal could conclude in the absence of an adequate explanation that the person against whom the claim is made (the respondent) has acted unlawfully, and

- the respondent fails to prove that he did not act in that way.

A disabled employee scores very poorly in a redundancy selection process in comparison with other employees in the same position as himself, getting low marks for skill and performance in his job. The employee has always had good appraisals in comparison with other employees and no action has ever been taken against him in respect of competence. Unless the employer demonstrates a non-discriminatory reason for the low scores, unlawful discrimination will be inferred in these circumstances.

4.43 Consequently, where a disabled person is able to prove on the balance of probabilities facts from which an inference of unlawful discrimination or harassment could be drawn, the burden of proof shifts to the respondent – for example, the disabled person's employer. This means that the employer must show that it is more likely than not that its conduct was not unlawful. This principle applies to allegations in respect of all forms of discrimination, including victimisation, and to harassment. Its practical effect in relation to the three principal forms of disability discrimination can be summarised as follows:

- To prove an allegation of **direct discrimination**, an employee must prove facts from which it could be inferred in the absence of an adequate explanation that he has been treated less favourably on the ground of his disability than an appropriate comparator has been, or would be, treated. If the employee does this, the claim will succeed unless the employer can show that disability was not any part of the reason for the treatment in question.

- To prove an allegation that there has been a **failure to comply with a duty to make reasonable adjustments**, an employee must prove facts from which it could be inferred in the absence of an adequate explanation that such a duty has arisen, and that it has been breached. If the employee does this, the claim will succeed unless the employer can show that it did not fail to comply with its duty in this regard.

- To prove an allegation of **disability-related discrimination**, an employee must prove facts from which it could be inferred in the absence of an adequate explanation that, for a reason relating to his disability, he has been treated less favourably than a person to whom that reason does not apply has been, or would be, treated. If the employee does this, the burden of proof shifts, and it is for the employer to show that the employee has not received less favourable treatment for a disability-related reason. Even if the employer cannot show this, however, the employee's claim will not succeed if the employer shows that the treatment was justified.

s 56
4.44 The Act provides a means by which a disabled person can seek evidence about whether he has been discriminated against, or subjected to harassment, under the Act's provisions on employment and occupation. He may do this by using a questionnaire to obtain further information from a person he thinks has acted unlawfully in relation to him (see paragraph 13.13). If there has been a failure to provide a satisfactory response to questions asked by the disabled person in this way, inferences may be drawn from that failure.

4.45 In addition, the fact that there has been a failure to comply with a relevant provision of the Code must be taken into account by a court or tribunal, where it considers it relevant, in determining whether there has been discrimination or harassment (see paragraph 1.6).

4

Introduction

5.1 In Chapter 4 it was noted that one of the ways in which discrimination occurs under Part 2 of the Act is when an employer fails to comply with a duty imposed on it to make 'reasonable adjustments' in relation to the disabled person. This chapter examines the circumstances in which a duty to make reasonable adjustments arises and outlines what an employer needs to do in order to discharge such a duty.

5.2 The concept of a duty to make reasonable adjustments is also relevant to the application of Part 2 in other situations – for example, in relation to the occupations mentioned in Chapter 9, and to the provision of occupational pensions, as explained in Chapter 10.

When does an employer's duty to make reasonable adjustments arise?

5.3 The duty to make reasonable adjustments arises where a provision, criterion or practice applied by or on behalf of the employer, or any physical feature of premises occupied by the employer, places a disabled person at a substantial disadvantage compared with people who are not disabled. An employer has to take such steps as it is reasonable for it to have to take in all the circumstances to prevent that disadvantage – in other words the employer has to make a

s 4A(1)

'reasonable adjustment'. Where the duty arises, an employer cannot justify a failure to make a reasonable adjustment.

> A man who is disabled because he has dyslexia applies for a job which involves writing letters. The employer gives all applicants a test of their letter-writing ability. The man can generally write letters very well but finds it difficult to do so in stressful situations and within short deadlines. He is given longer to take the test. This adjustment is likely to be a reasonable one for the employer to make.

5.4 It does not matter if a disabled person cannot point to an actual non-disabled person compared with whom he is at a substantial disadvantage. The fact that a non-disabled person, or even another disabled person, would not be substantially disadvantaged by the provision, criterion or practice or by the physical feature in question is irrelevant. The duty is owed specifically to the individual disabled person.

Which disabled people does the duty protect?

s 4A(2)

5.5 The duty to make reasonable adjustments applies in recruitment and during all stages of employment, including dismissal. It may also apply after employment has ended. The duty relates to all disabled employees of an employer and to any disabled applicant for employment. In the case of a provision, criterion or practice for determining to whom employment should be offered, the duty also applies in respect of any disabled person who has notified the employer that he may be an applicant for that employment.

5.6 The extent of the duty to make reasonable adjustments depends on the employment circumstances of the disabled person in question. For example, more extensive duties are owed to employees than to people who are merely thinking about applying for a job. More extensive duties are also owed to current employees than to former employees. The extent to which employers have knowledge of relevant circumstances is also a factor (see paragraphs 5.12 to 5.16).

5.7 In order to avoid discrimination, it would be prudent for employers not to attempt to make a fine judgement as to whether a particular individual falls within the statutory definition of disability, but to focus instead on meeting the needs of each employee and job applicant.

What are 'provisions, criteria and practices'?

5.8 Provisions, criteria and practices include arrangements, for example for determining to whom employment should be offered, and terms, conditions or arrangements on which employment, promotion, a transfer, training or any other benefit is offered or afforded. The duty to make reasonable adjustments applies, for example, to selection and interview procedures and the premises used for such procedures, as well as to job offers, contractual arrangements and working conditions.

s 18D(2)

> A call centre normally employs supervisors on a full-time basis. A woman with sickle cell anaemia applies for a job as a supervisor. Because of pain and fatigue relating to her condition she asks to be able to do the job on a part-time basis. The

5

call centre agrees. The hours of work which are offered amount to an adjustment to a working practice. This is likely to be a reasonable adjustment to the call centre's working practice.

An employer has a policy that designated car parking spaces are only offered to senior managers. A woman who is not a manager, but who has a mobility impairment and needs to park very close to the office, is given a designated car parking space. This is likely to be a reasonable adjustment to the employer's car parking policy.

What is a 'physical feature'?

s 18D(2)

5.9 The Act says that the following are to be treated as a physical feature:

■ any feature arising from the design or construction of a building on the premises occupied by the employer

■ any feature on the premises of any approach to, exit from, or access to such a building

■ any fixtures, fittings, furnishings, furniture, equipment or materials in or on the premises, and

■ any other physical element or quality of any land comprised in the premises occupied by the employer.

All these features are covered, whether temporary or permanent. Considerations which need to be taken into account when making adjustments to premises are explained in Chapter 12.

> The design of a particular workplace makes it difficult for someone with a hearing impairment to hear, because the main office is open plan and has hard flooring. That is a substantial disadvantage caused by the physical features of the workplace.

> Clear glass doors at the end of a corridor in a particular workplace present a hazard for a visually impaired employee. This is a substantial disadvantage caused by the physical features of the workplace.

5.10 Physical features will include steps, stairways, kerbs, exterior surfaces and paving, parking areas, building entrances and exits (including emergency escape routes), internal and external doors, gates, toilet and washing facilities, lighting and ventilation, lifts and escalators, floor coverings, signs, furniture, and temporary or movable items. This is not an exhaustive list.

What disadvantages give rise to the duty?

5.11 The Act says that only substantial disadvantages give rise to the duty. Substantial disadvantages are those which are not minor or trivial. Whether or not such a disadvantage exists in a particular case is a question of fact. What matters is not that a provision, criterion or practice or a physical feature is capable of causing a substantial disadvantage to the disabled person in question, but that it actually has this effect on him, or (where applicable) that it would have this effect if he were doing the job at the time.

What if the employer does not know that the person is disabled or is an actual or potential job applicant?

s 4A(3)(b)

5.12 Although (as explained in paragraphs 4.11 and 4.31) less favourable treatment can occur even if the employer does not know that an employee is disabled, the employer only has a duty to make an adjustment if it knows, or could reasonably be expected to know, that the employee has a disability and is likely to be placed at a substantial disadvantage. The employer must, however, do all it can reasonably be expected to do to find out whether this is the case.

> An employee has depression which sometimes causes her to cry at work, but the reason for her behaviour is not known to her employer. The employer makes no effort to find out if the employee is disabled and whether a reasonable adjustment could be made to her working arrangements. The employee is disciplined without being given any opportunity to explain that the problem arises from a disability. The employer may be in breach of the duty to make reasonable adjustments because it failed to do all it could reasonably be expected to do to establish if the employee was disabled and substantially disadvantaged.

> An employer has an annual appraisal system which specifically provides an opportunity for employees to notify the employer in confidence if they are disabled and are put at a substantial disadvantage by the working arrangements or premises. This gives the employer the opportunity to find out if an employee requires

reasonable adjustments, although it would not mean that the employer should not consider reasonable adjustments for an employee at other times of the year.

5.13 The principle stated in paragraph 5.12 applies equally to a disabled person who is an actual or potential applicant for employment.

s 4A(3)

An applicant is not short-listed for interview for the position of administrative assistant, a post which mainly involves typing, because he states on his application form that he cannot type. The reason he cannot type is that he has severe arthritis, but this is not stated anywhere on the form. The employer would not be expected to make an adjustment to the typing requirement in these circumstances as it had no knowledge of the disability and could not reasonably be expected to know of it.

5.14 In addition, an employer only has a duty to make an adjustment if it knows, or could reasonably be expected to know, that the disabled person is, or may be, an applicant.

5.15 If an employer's agent or employee (such as an occupational health adviser, a personnel officer or line manager or recruitment agent) knows, in that capacity, of an employee's disability, the employer will not usually be able to claim that it does not know of the disability, and that it therefore has no obligation to make a reasonable adjustment. The same applies in respect of actual or potential applicants for employment. Employers therefore need to ensure that where information about disabled people may come through different

5

channels, there is a means - suitably confidential - for bringing the information together, to make it easier for the employer to fulfil its duties under the Act.

An occupational health adviser is engaged by a large employer to provide it with information about its employees' health. The occupational health adviser becomes aware of an employee's disability, which the employee's line manager does not know about. The employer's working arrangements put the employee at a substantial disadvantage because of the effects of her disability and she claims that a reasonable adjustment should have been made. It will not be a defence for the employer to claim that it did not know of her disability. This is because the information gained by the occupational health adviser on the employer's behalf is imputed to the employer. The occupational health adviser's knowledge means that the employer's duty under the Act applies. If the employee did not give consent for the occupational health adviser to pass on personal information to the line manager, it might be necessary for the line manager to implement the reasonable adjustment without knowing precisely why it has to do so.

5.16 Information will not be imputed to the employer if it is gained by a person providing services to employees independently of the employer. This is the case even if the employer has arranged for those services to be provided.

An employer contracts with an agency to provide an independent counselling service to employees. The contract says that the counsellors are not acting on the employer's behalf while in the counselling role. Any information about a person's disability obtained by a counsellor during such counselling would not be imputed to the employer and so would not trigger the employer's duty to make reasonable adjustments.

Does the duty to make reasonable adjustments apply in other situations related to employment and occupation?

5.17 Paragraphs 5.3 to 5.16 explain when it may be necessary to make an adjustment in relation to employment. Part 2 imposes similar requirements in relation to the occupations it covers, subject to certain differences explained in Chapter 9. Reasonable adjustments may also be required in relation to occupational pension schemes and group insurance services, as explained in Chapter 10.

What adjustments might an employer have to make?

5.18 The Act gives a number of examples of adjustments, or 'steps', which employers may have to take, if it is reasonable for them to have to do so (see paragraphs 5.24 to 5.42). Any necessary adjustments should be implemented in a timely fashion, and it may also be necessary for an employer to make more than one adjustment. It is advisable to agree any proposed adjustments with the disabled person in question before they are made. The Act does not give an exhaustive list of the steps which may have to be taken to discharge the duty. Steps other than those listed

s 18B(2)

here, or a combination of steps, will sometimes have to be taken. However, the steps in the Act are:

■ making adjustments to premises

> An employer makes structural or other physical changes such as widening a doorway, providing a ramp or moving furniture for a wheelchair user; relocates light switches, door handles or shelves for someone who has difficulty in reaching; or provides appropriate contrast in decor to help the safe mobility of a visually impaired person.

■ allocating some of the disabled person's duties to another person

> An employer reallocates minor or subsidiary duties to another employee as a disabled person has difficulty doing them because of his disability. For example, the job involves occasionally going onto the open roof of a building but the employer transfers this work away from an employee whose disability involves severe vertigo.

■ transferring the person to fill an existing vacancy

> An employer should consider whether a suitable alternative post is available for an employee who becomes disabled (or whose disability worsens), where no reasonable adjustment would enable the employee to continue doing the current job. Such a post might also involve retraining or other reasonable adjustments such as equipment for the new post.

5

- altering the person's hours of working or training

This could include allowing a disabled person to work flexible hours to enable him to have additional breaks to overcome fatigue arising from his disability. It could also include permitting part time working, or different working hours to avoid the need to travel in the rush hour if this is a problem related to an impairment. A phased return to work with a gradual build-up of hours might also be appropriate in some circumstances.

- assigning the person to a different place of work or training

An employer relocates the work station of a newly disabled employee (who now uses a wheelchair) from an inaccessible third floor office to an accessible one on the ground floor. It would be reasonable to move his place of work to other premises of the same employer if the first building is inaccessible.

- allowing the person to be absent during working or training hours for rehabilitation, assessment or treatment

An employer allows a person who has become disabled more time off during work than would be allowed to non-disabled employees to enable him to have rehabilitation training. A similar adjustment would be appropriate if a disability worsens or if a disabled person needs occasional treatment anyway.

- giving, or arranging for, training or mentoring (whether for the disabled person or any other person)

> This could be training in particular pieces of equipment which the disabled person uses, or an alteration to the standard employee training to reflect the employee's particular disability. For example, all employees are trained in the use of a particular machine but an employer provides slightly different or longer training for an employee with restricted hand or arm movements, or training in additional software for a visually impaired person so that he can use a computer with speech output.

> An employer provides training for employees on conducting meetings in a way that enables a deaf staff member to participate effectively.

> A disabled man returns to work after a six-month period of absence due to a stroke. His employer pays for him to see a work mentor, and allows time off to see the mentor, to help with his loss of confidence following the onset of his disability.

- acquiring or modifying equipment

> An employer might have to provide special equipment (such as an adapted keyboard for someone with arthritis or a large screen for a visually impaired person), an adapted telephone for someone with a hearing impairment, or other modified equipment for disabled employees

5

(such as longer handles on a machine). There is no requirement to provide or modify equipment for personal purposes unconnected with an employee's work, such as providing a wheelchair if a person needs one in any event but does not have one. The disadvantage in such a case does not flow from the employer's arrangements or premises.

- modifying instructions or reference manuals

The format of instructions and manuals might need to be modified for some disabled people (e.g. produced in Braille or on audio tape) and instructions for people with learning disabilities might need to be conveyed orally with individual demonstration.

- modifying procedures for testing or assessment

A person with restricted manual dexterity would be disadvantaged by a written test, so the employer gives that person an oral test instead.

- providing a reader or interpreter

A colleague reads mail to a person with a visual impairment at particular times during the working day. Alternatively, the employer might hire a reader.

- providing supervision or other support

> An employer provides a support worker, or arranges help from a colleague, in appropriate circumstances, for someone whose disability leads to uncertainty or lack of confidence.

5.19 It may sometimes be necessary for an employer to take a combination of steps.

> A woman who is deafblind is given a new job with her employer in an unfamiliar part of the building. The employer (i) arranges facilities for her guide dog in the new area, (ii) arranges for her new instructions to be in Braille and (iii) trains colleagues to communicate with her, and provides disability equality training to all staff.

5.20 As mentioned above, it might be reasonable for employers to have to take other steps, which are not given as examples in the Act. These steps could include:

- conducting a proper assessment of what reasonable adjustments may be required

- permitting flexible working

- allowing a disabled employee to take a period of disability leave

> An employee who has cancer needs to undergo treatment and rehabilitation. His employer allows a period of disability leave and permits him to return to his job at the end of this period.

- participating in supported employment schemes, such as Workstep

A man applies for a job as an office assistant after several years of not working because of depression. He has been participating in a supported employment scheme where he saw the post advertised. As a reasonable adjustment he asks the employer to let him make private phone calls during the working day to a support worker at the scheme.

- employing a support worker to assist a disabled employee

An adviser with a visual impairment is sometimes required to make home visits. The employer employs a support worker to assist her on these visits.

- modifying disciplinary or grievance procedures

A woman with a learning disability is allowed to take a friend (who does not work with her) to act as an advocate at a meeting with her employer about a grievance. The employer also ensures that the meeting is conducted in a way that does not disadvantage or patronise the disabled woman.

- adjusting redundancy selection criteria

A woman with an autoimmune disease has taken several short periods of absence during the year because of the condition. When her employer is taking absences into account as a criterion for selecting people for redundancy, he discounts these periods of disability-related absence.

- modifying performance-related pay arrangements.

> A disabled woman who is paid purely on her output needs frequent short additional breaks during her working day – something her employer agrees to as a reasonable adjustment. It is likely to be a reasonable adjustment for her employer to pay her at an agreed rate (e.g. her average hourly rate) for these breaks.

5.21 Advice and assistance (which may include financial assistance) in relation to making adjustments may be available from the Access to Work scheme (see paragraphs 8.19 and 8.20).

5.22 In some cases a reasonable adjustment will not work without the co-operation of other employees. Employees may therefore have an important role in helping to ensure that a reasonable adjustment is carried out in practice. Subject to considerations about confidentiality (explained at paragraphs 8.21 to 8.23), employers must ensure that this happens. It is unlikely to be a valid defence to a claim under the Act that staff were obstructive or unhelpful when the employer tried to make reasonable adjustments. An employer would at least need to be able to show that it took such behaviour seriously and dealt with it appropriately. Employers will be more likely to be able to do this if they establish and implement the type of policies and practices described at paragraph 2.12.

> An employer ensures that an employee with autism has a structured working day as a reasonable adjustment. As part of the reasonable adjustment it is the responsibility of the employer to ensure that other employees co-operate with this arrangement.

5.23 Further examples of the way in which reasonable adjustments work in practice are given in Chapters 7 and 8, which deal with recruitment and retention.

When is it 'reasonable' for an employer to have to make adjustments?

5.24 Whether it is reasonable for an employer to make any particular adjustment will depend on a number of things, such as its cost and effectiveness. However, if an adjustment is one which it is reasonable to make, then the employer must do so. Where a disabled person is placed at a substantial disadvantage by a provision, criterion or practice of the employer, or by a physical feature of the premises it occupies, the employer must consider whether any reasonable adjustments can be made to overcome that disadvantage. There is no onus on the disabled person to suggest what adjustments should be made (although it is good practice for employers to ask) but, where the disabled person does so, the employer must consider whether such adjustments would help overcome the disadvantage, and whether they are reasonable.

A disabled employee has been absent from work as a result of depression. Neither the employee nor his doctor is able to suggest any adjustments that could be made. Nevertheless the employer should still consider whether any adjustments, such as working from home for a time, would be reasonable.

5.25 Effective and practicable adjustments for disabled people often involve little or no cost or disruption and are therefore very likely to be reasonable for an employer to have to make. Even if an adjustment has a significant cost associated with it, it may still be cost-effective in overall terms – and so may be a reasonable adjustment to make. Many adjustments do not involve making physical changes to premises. However, where such changes do need to be made, employers may need to take account of the considerations explained in Chapter 12 which deals with issues about making alterations to premises.

SI 1999/3242

5.26 If making a particular adjustment would increase the risks to the health and safety of any person (including the disabled person in question) then this is a relevant factor in deciding whether it is reasonable to make that adjustment. Suitable and sufficient risk assessments, such as those carried out for the purposes of the Management of Health and Safety at Work Regulations 1999, should be used to help determine whether such risks are likely to arise.

s 18B(1)

5.27 The Act lists a number of factors which may, in particular, have a bearing on whether it will be reasonable for the employer to have to make a particular adjustment. These factors make a useful checklist, particularly when considering more substantial adjustments. The effectiveness and practicability of a particular adjustment might be considered first. If it is practicable and effective, the financial aspects might be looked at as a whole – the cost of the adjustment and resources available to fund it. Other factors might also have a bearing. The factors in the Act are listed below.

The effectiveness of the step in preventing the disadvantage

5.28 It is unlikely to be reasonable for an employer to have to make an adjustment involving little benefit to the disabled person.

> A disabled employee cannot physically access the stationery cupboard at work. It is unlikely to be reasonable for the employer to have to make the cupboard accessible, unless distribution of stationery was a significant part of the employee's job.

5.29 However, an adjustment which, taken alone, is of marginal benefit, may be one of several adjustments which, when looked at together, would be effective. In that case, it is likely to be reasonable to have to make it.

The practicability of the step

5.30 It is more likely to be reasonable for an employer to have to take a step which is easy to take than one which is difficult. In some circumstances it may be reasonable to have to take a step, even though it is difficult.

> It might be impracticable for an employer who needs to appoint an employee urgently to have to wait for an adjustment to be made to an entrance. How long it might be reasonable for the employer to have to wait would depend on the circumstances. However, it might be possible to make a temporary adjustment in the meantime, such as using another, less convenient entrance.

The financial and other costs of the adjustment and the extent of any disruption caused

5.31 If an adjustment costs little or nothing and is not disruptive, it would be reasonable unless some other factor (such as practicability or effectiveness) made it unreasonable. The costs to be taken into account include those for staff and other resources. The significance of the cost of a step may depend in part on what the employer might otherwise spend in the circumstances. In assessing the likely costs of making an adjustment, the availability of external funding (such as funding by Access to Work) should be taken into account.

> It would be reasonable for an employer to have to spend at least as much on an adjustment to enable the retention of a disabled person - including any retraining - as might be spent on recruiting and training a replacement.

5.32 The significance of the cost of a step may also depend in part on the value of the employee's experience and expertise to the employer.

5.33 Examples of the factors that might be considered as relating to the value of an employee would include:

- the amount of resources (such as training) invested in the individual by the employer

- the employee's length of service

- the employee's level of skill and knowledge

- the employee's quality of relationships with clients

- the level of the employee's pay.

5.34 It is more likely to be reasonable for an employer to have to make an adjustment with significant costs for an employee who is likely to be in the job for some time than for a temporary employee.

5.35 An employer is more likely to have to make an adjustment which might cause only minor inconvenience to other employees or the employer than one which might unavoidably prevent other employees from doing their job, or cause other significant disruption.

The extent of the employer's financial or other resources

5.36 It is more likely to be reasonable for an employer with substantial financial resources to have to make an adjustment with a significant cost, than for an employer with fewer resources. The resources in practice available to the employer as a whole should be taken into account as well as other calls on those resources. For larger employers, it is good practice to have a specific budget for reasonable adjustments – but limitations on the size of any such budget will not affect the existence of the employer's duties to disabled employees. The reasonableness of an adjustment will depend not only on the resources in practice available for the adjustment but also on all other relevant factors (such as effectiveness and practicability).

> If a shop is part of a retail chain, the total resources of that business would be taken into account when assessing whether an adjustment is reasonable. Competing demands on those resources will also be taken into account.

5.37 It is more likely to be reasonable for an employer with a substantial number of staff to have to make certain adjustments, than for a smaller employer.

It would generally be reasonable for an employer with a large staff to make significant efforts to reallocate duties or identify a suitable alternative post or provide supervision from existing staff. It may also be reasonable for a small company to make these adjustments but not if it involved disproportionate effort.

The availability to the employer of financial or other assistance to help make an adjustment

5.38 The availability of outside help (such as advice and assistance from Access to Work) may well be a relevant factor.

A small employer, in recruiting a disabled person, finds that the only feasible adjustment is too costly for it alone. However, if assistance is available e.g. from the Access to Work scheme or a voluntary body, it may well be reasonable for the employer to make the adjustment.

5.39 A disabled person is not required to contribute to the cost of a reasonable adjustment. However, if a disabled person has a particular piece of special or adapted equipment which he is prepared to use for work, this might make it reasonable for the employer to have to take some other step (as well as allowing the use of the equipment).

An employer requires its employees to use company cars for all business travel. One employee's disability means she would have to use an adapted car or an alternative form of transport. If she has an adapted car of her own which she is willing to use on business, it might well be reasonable for the employer to allow this and pay her an allowance to cover the cost of doing so, even if it might not have been reasonable for it to provide an adapted company car (because of the additional expense), or to pay an allowance to cover alternative travel arrangements in the absence of an adapted car. This would be a reasonable step to take because it would be cost-effective for the employer, easy to implement and would remove the disadvantage to the disabled employee immediately.

A disabled woman employed as a computer engineer uses a piece of communications equipment that she obtained through the Access to Work scheme. Her employer pays the cost of repair when it breaks down.

The nature of the employer's activities, and the size of its undertaking

5.40 As explained in paragraphs 3.9 and 3.10, Part 2 now applies to all employers (except for the Armed Forces), irrespective of their size. However, the size of an employer's undertaking and the nature of its activities may be relevant in determining the reasonableness of a particular step.

A small manufacturing company making chairs employs a craftswoman who becomes disabled and can no longer carry out her job, even after adjustments have been considered. The only jobs available in the company are production-based as the company owner herself carries out all other functions, such as marketing and running the office. Given the nature of the business, it is not likely to be reasonable for the employer to provide an alternative job for the employee.

In contrast, a business of the same size which designs, manufactures and retails games is likely to have a wide range of jobs. In these circumstances, if an employee were no longer able to work in a production role it might be reasonable for the employer to provide an alternative job.

A sales assistant in a small shop who has a mental health problem requests time off each week to attend a psychotherapy appointment. It would be more likely to be reasonable for her employer to agree to this if there were other sales assistants who could cover for her absence.

In relation to private households, the extent to which taking the step would disrupt the household or disturb any person residing there

5.41 The duty to make reasonable adjustments may apply in respect of disabled people who work in private households. However, even if the financial cost would be minimal, it might not be reasonable to take a particular step if doing so would entail disruption to the household or disturbance to people who live there.

A man employs a deaf cleaner in his house. They communicate with each other by writing notes. It is likely to be a reasonable adjustment for him to communicate with her in this way.

A person with a severe dust allergy applies for the position of nanny. When she is interviewed it becomes apparent that she can only work in an environment which is dust free. The prospective employers take the view that this would be too disruptive to their home life. It is unlikely to be reasonable for them to have to make the adjustments needed to employ this person.

Other factors

5.42 Although the Act does not mention any further factors, others may be relevant depending on the circumstances. For example:

■ effect on other employees

A disabled person wants to work in a cold office as heat aggravates his skin condition. This is not reasonable in the open plan office where he works because it would be uncomfortable for other employees to have to work in these conditions. Moving him to a small office on his own may be a reasonable adjustment in these circumstances.

A disabled woman working as a baker in a small bakery wants to avoid night shifts because disturbances to her sleep patterns trigger her migraines. Other employees would also like to avoid night shifts, for reasons unrelated to disability. This is unlikely to be a relevant factor for the employer in considering whether it is reasonable to allow the disabled employee's request.

■ adjustments made for other disabled employees

> If an employer has a number of staff with mobility problems this may mean that it would be reasonable to make significant structural changes to their workplace.

- the extent to which the disabled person is willing to co-operate

> An employee with a mobility impairment works in a team located on an upper floor to which there is no access by lift. Getting there is very tiring for the employee, and the employer could easily make a more accessible location available for him. Following a workplace assessment the employer decides to move the employee to the alternative location, but the employee refuses to co-operate. If there is no other adjustment that the employer can reasonably make, it does not have to do any more.

Can failure to make a reasonable adjustment ever be justified?

s 3A(2)

5.43 The Act does not permit an employer to justify a failure to comply with a duty to make a reasonable adjustment. This is a change in the law (see Appendix A).

5.44 Clearly, however, an employer will only breach such a duty if the adjustment in question is one which it is reasonable for it to have to make. So, where the duty applies, it is the question of 'reasonableness' which alone determines whether the adjustment has to be made.

Introduction

6.1 Most conduct which is potentially unlawful under Part 2 of the Act cannot be justified. Conduct which amounts to:

- direct discrimination

- failure to comply with a duty to make a reasonable adjustment

- victimisation

- harassment

- instructions or pressure to discriminate, or

- aiding an unlawful act

is unlawful irrespective of the reason or motive for it.

When does the Act permit justification?

6.2 Paragraph 4.27 explains that one of the forms of discrimination which is unlawful under Part 2 is disability-related discrimination. However, an employer's conduct towards a disabled person does not amount to disability-related discrimination if it can be justified. This chapter explains the limited circumstances in which this may happen.

6.3 Where less favourable treatment of a disabled person is capable of being justified (that is, where it is **not** direct discrimination), the Act says that it will, in fact, be justified if, but only if, the reason for the treatment is both material to the circumstances of the particular case **and** substantial. This is an objective test. 'Material' means that there must be a reasonably strong connection between the reason given for the treatment and the circumstances of the particular case. 'Substantial' means, in the context of justification, that the reason must carry real weight and be of substance.

> A man who has severe back pain and is unable to bend is rejected for a job as a carpet fitter as he cannot carry out the essential requirement of the job, which is to fit carpets. This would be lawful as the reason he is rejected is a substantial one and is clearly material to the circumstances.

6.4 In certain circumstances, the existence of a material and substantial reason for disability-related less favourable treatment is not enough to justify that treatment. This is the case where an employer is also under a duty to make reasonable adjustments in relation to the disabled person but fails to comply with that duty.

s 3A(6)

6.5 In those circumstances, it is necessary to consider not only whether there is a material and substantial reason for the less favourable treatment, but also whether the treatment would still have been justified even if the employer had complied with its duty to make reasonable adjustments. In effect, it is necessary to ask the question 'would a reasonable adjustment have made any difference?' If a reasonable adjustment would have made a difference to the reason that is being used to justify the treatment, then the less favourable treatment cannot be justified.

An applicant for an administrative job appears not to be the best person for the job, but only because her typing speed is too slow as a result of arthritis in her hands. If a reasonable adjustment - perhaps an adapted keyboard - would overcome this, her typing speed would not in itself be a substantial reason for not employing her. Therefore the employer would be unlawfully discriminating if, on account of her typing speed, he did not employ her or provide that adjustment.

6.6 In relation to disability-related discrimination, the fact that an employer has failed to comply with a duty to make a reasonable adjustment means that the sequence of events for justifying disability-related less favourable treatment is as follows:

- The disabled person proves facts from which it could be inferred in the absence of an adequate explanation that:

  a. for a reason related to his disability, he has been treated less favourably than a person to whom that reason does not apply has been, or would be, treated, and

  b. a duty to make a reasonable adjustment has arisen in respect of him and the employer has failed to comply with it.

- The employer will be found to have discriminated unless it proves that:

  a. the reason for the treatment is both material to the circumstances of the particular case and substantial, and

  b. the reason would still have applied if the reasonable adjustment had been made.

Can health and safety concerns justify less favourable treatment?

6.7 Stereotypical assumptions about the health and safety implications of disability should be avoided, both in general terms and in relation to particular types of disability. Indeed, less favourable treatment which is based on such assumptions may itself amount to direct discrimination – which is incapable of justification (see paragraph 4.5). The fact that a person has a disability does not necessarily mean that he represents an additional risk to health and safety.

An employer has a policy of not employing anyone with diabetes because it believes that people with this condition are a health and safety risk. A person with diabetes applies to work for this employer and is turned down on the basis of her disability, without regard to her personal circumstances. A stereotypical assumption has been made which is likely to amount to direct discrimination and is therefore unlawful.

6.8 Under health and safety law it is the duty of every employer to ensure, so far as is reasonably practicable, the health, safety and welfare at work of all employees. Part of this duty is a requirement for all employers to assess the risks to the health and safety of all employees in the workplace and then to put in place measures that reduce the risks to as low a level as can reasonably be achieved. Genuine concerns about the health and safety of anybody (including a disabled employee) may be relevant when seeking to establish that disability-related less favourable treatment of a disabled person is justified. However, it is important to remember that health and safety law does not require employers to remove all conceivable risk, but to ensure that risk is properly appreciated, understood and managed. Further information can be obtained from the Health and Safety Executive (see Appendix C for details).

6.9 It is the employer who must decide what action to take in response to concerns about health and safety. However, when an employer has reason to think that the effects of a person's disability may give rise to an issue about health and safety, it is prudent for it to have a new risk assessment carried out by a suitably qualified person. This is because:

- If an employer treats a disabled person less favourably merely on the basis of generalised assumptions about the health and safety implications of having a disability, such treatment may itself amount to direct discrimination – which is incapable of justification.

- Even where there is no direct discrimination, an employer which treats a disabled person less favourably without having a suitable and sufficient risk assessment carried out is unlikely to be able to show that its concerns about health and safety justify the less favourable treatment.

> A pilot develops a heart condition, and his employer asks him to undertake a risk assessment to be carried out by an appropriate consultant. This is likely to be justifiable.

6.10 Nevertheless, an employer should not subject a disabled person to a risk assessment if this is not merited by the particular circumstances of the case.

A person with a learning disability has been working in a shop for many years, stocking shelves without any problems. A new manager is appointed who insists that a risk assessment is carried out for her but not for all the other shelf stackers. This is unlikely to be warranted – and indeed it is likely to amount to direct discrimination.

6.11 A risk assessment must be suitable and sufficient. It should identify the risks associated with a work activity, taking account of any reasonable adjustments put in place for the disabled person, and should be specific for the individual carrying out a particular task. It is therefore unlikely that an employer which has a **general** policy of treating people with certain disabilities (such as epilepsy, diabetes or mental health problems) less favourably than other people will be able to justify doing so – even if that policy is in accordance with the advice of an occupational health adviser.

6.12 A 'blanket' policy of this nature will usually be unlawful. This is because it is likely to amount to direct discrimination (which cannot ever be justified) or to disability-related less favourable treatment which is not justifiable in the circumstances - ie disability-related discrimination (see paragraphs 7.8 and 7.9).

6.13 Reasonable adjustments made by an employer may remove or reduce health and safety risks related to a person's disability. A suitable and sufficient assessment of such risks therefore needs to take account of the impact which making any reasonable adjustments would have. If a risk assessment is not conducted on this basis, then an employer is unlikely to be able to show that its concerns about health and safety justify less favourable treatment of the disabled person.

6

Can medical information justify less favourable treatment?

6.14 Consideration of medical information (such as a doctor's report or the answers to a medical questionnaire) is likely to form part of an assessment of health and safety risks. In most cases, however, having a disability does not adversely affect a person's general health. In other cases, its effect on a person's health may fluctuate. Although medical information about a disability may justify an adverse employment decision (such as a decision to dismiss or not to promote), it will not do so if there is no effect on the person's ability to do the job (or if any effect is less than substantial), no matter how great the effects of the disability are in other ways. Indeed, less favourable treatment of a disabled person in a case where his disability has no effect on his ability to do the job may well amount to direct discrimination – which is incapable of being justified.

An employer requires all candidates for a job as a technician in a chemical plant to complete a medical questionnaire. Medical information about one candidate shows that she has a degenerative condition which is likely to affect her ability to walk. This is not relevant to her ability to do the sedentary job in question. It would be unlawful for the employer to reject her on the ground of her disability as her disability is irrelevant to her ability to do the job. This would amount to direct discrimination.

The same employer is looking for a technician to work on a specific project for two years. A medical questionnaire shows that a candidate has a degenerative condition which could mean that he would not be able to work for that long. Because of this, further medical evidence is requested from his doctor and this confirms that he would not be able to work for two years. It is likely to be lawful to reject this candidate if the two-year requirement is justified in terms of the work and if there are no reasonable adjustments that could be made.

6.15 In addition, where medical information is available, employers must weigh it up in the context of the actual job, and the capabilities of the individual. An employer should also consider whether reasonable adjustments could be made in order to overcome any problems which may have been identified as a result of the medical information. It should not be taken for granted that the person who provides the medical information will be aware that employers have a duty to make reasonable adjustments, what these adjustments might be, or of the relevant working arrangements. It is good practice, therefore, to ensure that medical advisers are made aware of these matters. Information provided by a medical adviser should only be relied on if the adviser has the appropriate knowledge and expertise.

An occupational health adviser recommends that an administrative assistant cannot carry on in her current job because she has been diagnosed with Repetitive Strain Injury. The employer has another member of staff who uses voice recognition software, and considers this technology may be of relevance. The employer asks the adviser to review his conclusion taking this into account. The adviser revises his opinion and concludes that, with appropriate software, she can continue in her role.

6.16 In any event, although medical evidence may generally be considered as an 'expert contribution', it should not ordinarily be the sole factor influencing an employer's decision on employment related matters. The views of the disabled person (about his own capabilities and possible adjustments) should also be sought. In addition, and subject to the considerations about confidentiality explained in paragraphs 8.21 and 8.22, other contributions could come from the disabled person's line manager (about the nature of the job and possible adjustments). It may also be possible to seek help from disability organisations or from Jobcentre Plus, who have staff trained to advise about disability issues in the workplace. Ultimately, it is for the employer – and not the medical adviser – to take decisions as to whether, for example, to reject a job applicant or to maintain a disabled person's employment.

An employer receives advice from an occupational health adviser stating simply that an employee is 'unfit for work'. In spite of this the employer must consider whether there are reasonable adjustments which should be made.

7 Discrimination in the recruitment of employees

Introduction

7.1 It has already been explained (at paragraph 3.18) that it is unlawful for an employer to discriminate against a disabled person:

s 4(1)

- in the arrangements made for determining who should be offered employment

- in the terms on which the disabled person is offered employment, or

- by refusing to offer, or deliberately not offering, the disabled person employment.

7.2 This chapter examines these principles in more detail. In order to do so, it is necessary to look at the various stages of the recruitment process, from specifying the job and advertising the vacancy, to the process of assessing candidates, interview and selection.

7.3 Although the following paragraphs refer only to the recruitment of employees, it should be remembered that the same principles apply to the recruitment of people to occupations covered by the Act's provisions on employment and occupation. Any variations in the way the Act applies to such occupations are explained in Chapter 9.

General considerations

Recruiting the best person for the job

7.4 Before considering the recruitment process itself it should be noted that, although an employer must not discriminate against a disabled candidate, there is no requirement (aside from the duty to make reasonable adjustments) to treat a disabled person more favourably than it treats or would treat others. An employer will have to assess an applicant's merits as they would be if any reasonable adjustments required under the Act had been made. If, after allowing for those adjustments, a disabled person would not be the best person for the job, the employer does not have to recruit that person.

7.5 On the other hand, the Act does not prevent posts being advertised as open only to disabled applicants, or to an applicant being preferred for the job because of his disability. Special rules apply to local authority employers, however, as explained in paragraph 13.25.

A note about 'arrangements' for determining who should be offered employment

7.6 Although the statutory provisions specifically deal with recruitment in relation to employment as defined by the Act (see paragraph 3.8), the meaning of 'arrangements' – that is, arrangements for determining who should be offered employment – is wide. Such arrangements are not confined to those which an employer makes in deciding who should be offered a specific job, but also include arrangements for deciding who should be offered employment more generally. Thus, for example, participation in a pre-employment training programme could be 'an arrangement' if its completion is a necessary step along the road to gaining an offer of employment.

Specifying the job

How does the Act affect the way in which a job description or person specification should be prepared?

7.7 The inclusion of unnecessary or marginal requirements in a job description or person specification can lead to discrimination.

> An employer stipulates that employees must be 'active and energetic', when in fact the job in question is largely sedentary in nature. This requirement could unjustifiably exclude some people whose disabilities result in them getting tired more easily than others.

> An employer specifies that a driving licence is required for a job which involves limited travel. An applicant for the job has no driving licence because of the particular effects in his case of cerebral palsy. He is otherwise the best candidate for that job, he could easily and cheaply do the travelling involved other than by driving and it is likely to be a reasonable adjustment for the employer to let him do so. It would be discriminatory to insist on the specification and reject his application solely because he has no driving licence.

> An employer stipulates that employees must be 'good team players', when in fact the job in question does not involve working in a team. This requirement could unjustifiably exclude some people who have difficulty communicating, such as some people with autism.

7.8 Blanket exclusions (i.e. exclusions which do not take account of individual circumstances) can also lead to discrimination. Indeed, such exclusions are likely to amount to direct discrimination, and so be incapable of justification (see paragraph 4.5).

An employer excludes people with epilepsy from all driving jobs. One of the jobs, in practice, only requires a standard licence and standard insurance cover. If, as a result, someone with epilepsy, who has such a licence and can obtain such insurance cover, is turned down for the job, the employer will have discriminated unlawfully in excluding her from consideration.

An employer stipulates that candidates for a job must not have a history of mental illness, believing that such candidates will have poor attendance. The employer rejects an applicant solely because he has had a mental illness, without checking the individual's actual attendance record. This will amount to discrimination – and will be unlawful.

An employer stipulates that anyone with an infectious disease cannot work in the food preparation area. It refuses to employ someone with AIDS in this area, believing him to be a health and safety risk. Whether or not the employer has a written policy to this effect, this action will amount to discrimination, as the employer has not considered the actual circumstances of the case.

7.9 In addition, stating that a certain personal, medical or health-related characteristic is essential or desirable can lead to discrimination if the characteristic is not necessary for the performance of the job. An employer would therefore need to ensure that any such requirements were genuinely essential to the job, and that it would not be reasonable to waive them in any individual case.

> A television company requires all television engineers to have a high standard of hearing and vision. A woman with a hearing impairment is turned down for a job in the graphic design department because she does not pass a hearing test. If this standard of hearing is not necessary in order to do the particular job she applied for, the employer will have unlawfully discriminated against her by failing to make a reasonable adjustment to its policy of requiring job applicants to pass the test.

7.10 Likewise, although an employer is entitled to specify that applicants for a job must have certain qualifications, it will have to justify rejecting a disabled person for lacking a qualification if the reason why the disabled person lacks it is related to his disability. Justification will involve showing that the qualification is relevant and significant in terms of the particular job and the particular applicant, and that there is no reasonable adjustment which would change this. In some circumstances it might be feasible to reassign the duties to which the qualification relates, or to waive the requirement for the qualification if this particular applicant has alternative evidence of the necessary level of competence.

An employer seeking someone to work in an administrative post specifies that candidates must have the relevant NVQ Level 4 qualification. If Level 4 fairly reflects the complex and varied nature and substantial personal responsibility of the work, and these aspects of the job cannot reasonably be altered, the employer will be able to justify rejecting a disabled applicant who has only been able to reach Level 3 because of his disability and who cannot show the relevant level of competence by other means.

An employer specifies that two GCSEs are required for a certain post. This is to show that a candidate has the general level of ability required. No particular subjects are specified. An applicant whose dyslexia prevented her from passing written examinations cannot meet this requirement. The employer would be unable to justify rejecting her on this account alone if she could show in some other way that she had the expertise called for in the post.

Advertising the vacancy

Can a job advertisement encourage applications from disabled people?

7.11 The Act does not prevent a job advertisement saying that the employer would welcome applications from disabled people. This would be a positive and public statement of the employer's policy. More information about good practice in relation to attracting disabled job applicants is given at paragraphs 2.17 and 2.18.

7.12 The Act says that, when advertising a job vacancy, it is unlawful for the person offering the job to publish an advertisement (or cause it to be published) which indicates, or might reasonably be understood to indicate:

s 16B(1)

■ that the success of a person's application for the job may depend to any extent on his not having any disability, or any particular disability, or

■ that the person determining the application is reluctant to make reasonable adjustments.

An employer advertises a work placement for an office worker, stating 'We are sorry but because our offices are on the first floor, they are not accessible to disabled people'. This is likely to be unlawful. It would be better for the advertisement to state 'although our offices are on the first floor, we welcome applications from disabled people and are willing to make reasonable adjustments.'

An advertisement for an assistant in office supplies stipulates that a driving licence is required. The post itself does not involve significant amounts of driving, and reasonable adjustments to this element of the job would be possible. However, the advertisement implies that the employer is unwilling to make such reasonable adjustments, for example by allowing travel by taxi or allocating the driving to someone else. This is likely to be unlawful.

7

7.13 This applies to every form of advertisement or notice, whether to the public or not, for any employment, promotion or transfer of employment. However, an advertisement may still be lawful even if it does indicate that having a particular disability will adversely affect an applicant's prospects of success. This will be the case where, for example, because of the nature of the job in question, the employer is entitled to take the effects of the disability into account when assessing the suitability of applicants.

> It would be lawful for a company specialising in inner city bicycle courier services to advertise for couriers who 'must be able to ride a bicycle.'

s 17B(1)

7.14 The Act does not give individual job applicants the right to take legal action in respect of discriminatory advertisements. Such action may only be taken by the DRC (see paragraphs 13.28 to 13.30).

> An employer states in an advertisement for an office worker, 'Sorry but gaining access to our building can be difficult for some people.' The DRC could take proceedings on the grounds that this constitutes a discriminatory advertisement.

7.15 In addition, it should be noted that the content of the advertisement could be taken into account by an employment tribunal in determining a claim brought by a disabled person under the Act.

> A disabled person who walks with the aid of crutches applies for the job mentioned in the previous example and is turned down. He could ask the employment tribunal to take the content

of the advertisement into account when determining whether he did not get the job for a disability-related reason.

Application forms and information

Does an employer have to provide information about jobs in accessible formats?

7.16 Where an employer provides information about a job, it is likely to be a reasonable adjustment for it to provide on request information in a format that is accessible to a disabled applicant – particularly if the employer's information systems, and the time available before the new employee is needed, mean it can easily be done. Accessible formats include email, Braille, Easy Read, large print, audio tape and computer disc. A disabled person's requirements will depend upon his impairment, but on other factors too. For example, many blind people do not read Braille but prefer to receive information by email or on audio tape.

A person whom the employer knows to be disabled asks to be given information about a job in a format that is accessible to her. It is likely to be a reasonable adjustment for the employer to provide the information in an accessible format.

An employer advertises vacancies on its website. The website is not accessible to disabled people who use particular types of software on their computers. A man with a visual impairment, who uses 'screen reader' software on his computer and has notified the employer that he would like to work for it, cannot read the job vacancies on

7

the employer's website. It is likely to be unlawful for the employer to refuse to make its website accessible to the disabled man, unless it is prepared to provide him with the same information in an accessible format.

Does an employer have to accept applications in accessible formats?

7.17 Where an employer invites applications by completing and returning an application form, it is likely to be a reasonable adjustment for it to accept applications which contain the necessary information in accessible formats. However, a disabled person might not have a right to submit an application in his preferred format (such as Braille) if he would not be substantially disadvantaged by submitting it in some other format (such as email) which the employer would find easier to access. Where applications are invited by completing and returning a form on-line, that form should be accessible to disabled people (or an accessible alternative should be provided).

Because of his disability, a candidate asks to submit an application in a particular format, different from the one specified for candidates in general (eg on tape). It is likely to be a reasonable adjustment for the employer to allow this.

7.18 Whether or not an application is submitted in an accessible format, employers and their staff or agents must not discriminate against disabled people in the way that they deal with their applications.

Selection, assessment and interview arrangements

When must an employer make adjustments to its selection, assessment and interview arrangements?

7.19 An employer is not required to make changes in anticipation of applications from disabled people in general – although it would obviously be good practice to do so. It is only if the employer knows or could be reasonably expected to know that a particular disabled person is, or may be, applying and is likely to be substantially disadvantaged by the employer's premises or arrangements, that the employer may have to make changes.

When should an employer short-list a disabled person for interview?

7.20 Many employers operate a guaranteed interview scheme, under which a disabled candidate who wishes to use the scheme will be short-listed for interview automatically if he demonstrates that he meets the minimum criteria for getting the job.

7.21 Regardless of whether an employer operates a guaranteed interview scheme, it will need to consider whether it should make reasonable adjustments when short-listing for interview. This will be the case if an employer knows or ought to know that an applicant has a disability and is likely to be at a substantial disadvantage because of its recruitment arrangements or the premises in which any interviews are held. In these circumstances, the employer should consider whether there is any reasonable adjustment which would remove the disadvantage. Any such adjustment should be taken into account when short-listing applicants. If the employer cannot make this judgment without more information it would be discriminatory for it not to put the disabled person on the short-list for

7

interview if that is how it would normally seek additional information about candidates.

What adjustments might an employer have to make when arranging or conducting interviews?

7.22 Employers should think ahead for interviews. Depending upon the circumstances, changes may need to be made to arrangements for interviews or to the way in which interviews are carried out.

A hearing impaired candidate informs a potential employer that he can lip read but will need to be able to see the interviewer's face clearly. The interviewer ensures that her face is well lit, that she faces the applicant when speaking, that she speaks clearly and is prepared to repeat questions if the candidate does not understand her. These are likely to be reasonable adjustments for the employer to make.

An employer arranges a British Sign Language (BSL) interpreter to attend an interview with a deaf candidate who uses BSL to communicate. The interviewer also allows extra time for the interview. (Communication support for interviews such as sign language interpreters may also be available through the Access to Work scheme). These are likely to be reasonable adjustments for the employer to make.

An employer pays expenses to candidates who come for interview. A disabled candidate brings his support worker with him to the interview. The employer pays the expenses of the support worker as well. This is likely to be a reasonable adjustment to the usual policy of paying only the candidate's own expenses.

7

An employer allows a candidate who has a learning disability to bring a supportive person to an interview to assist when answering questions that are not part of the assessment itself. This is likely to be a reasonable adjustment to the selection process.

7.23 It is a good idea to give applicants the opportunity to indicate any relevant effects of a disability and to suggest adjustments to help overcome any disadvantage the disability may cause at interview. This could help the employer avoid discrimination in the interview and in considering the application, by clarifying whether any reasonable adjustments may be required. However, an employer must not assume that no adjustments need to be made simply because the applicant has not requested any (see paragraph 5.24).

7.24 The practical effects of an employer's duties may be different if a person whom the employer previously did not know, and could not reasonably be expected to have known, to be disabled arrives for interview and is substantially disadvantaged because of the arrangements. The employer may still be under a duty to make a reasonable adjustment from the time that it first learns of the disability and the disadvantage. However, the employer might not be required to do as much as might have been the case if it had known (or if it ought to have known) in advance about the disability and its effects.

A job applicant does not tell an employer in advance that she uses a wheelchair and the employer does not know of her disability. On arriving for the interview she discovers that the room is not accessible. Although the employer could not have been expected to make the necessary changes in advance, it would be a reasonable adjustment to hold the interview in an alternative, accessible room if one was available without too much disruption or cost. Alternatively, it might be a reasonable adjustment to reschedule the interview if this was practicable.

What about aptitude or other tests in the recruitment process?

7.25 The Act does not prevent employers carrying out aptitude or other tests, including psychological tests. However, routine testing of all candidates may still discriminate against particular individuals or substantially disadvantage them. In those cases, the employer would need to revise the tests – or the way the results are assessed – to take account of a disabled candidate. This does not apply, however, where the nature and form of the test is necessary to assess a matter relevant to the job. The following are examples of adjustments which may be reasonable:

■ allowing a disabled person extra time to complete the test

■ permitting a disabled person the assistance of a reader or scribe during the test

■ accepting a lower 'pass rate' for a person whose disability inhibits performance in such a test.

The extent to which such adjustments might be required would depend on how closely the test is related to the job in question and what adjustments the employer might have to make if the applicant were given the job.

> An employer sets a word processing test for candidates for a position as administrative officer. A person with repetitive strain injury (RSI) takes the test using voice-activated software, as this is how she would carry out the job if she were appointed. Permitting her to take the test in this way is likely to be a reasonable adjustment for the employer to make.

> An employer sets candidates a short oral test. An applicant is disabled by a severe stammer, but only under stress. It is likely to be a reasonable adjustment to allow her more time to complete the test. Alternatively, it may be a reasonable adjustment to give the test in written form instead – though not if excellent oral communication skills are necessary for the job and assessing those skills was the purpose of the test.

7.26 However, employers would be well advised to seek professional advice in the light of individual circumstances before making adjustments to psychological or aptitude tests.

When can an employer ask questions about a disability?

7.27 The Act does not prohibit an employer from seeking information about a disability. However, the Data Protection Code of Practice on Employment and Recruitment (see Appendix C for details) states that information should not be sought from applicants unless necessary to enable the recruitment decision to be made, or for a related purpose such as equal opportunities monitoring. Disability-related questions must not be used to discriminate against a disabled person.

An employer should only ask such questions if they are, or may be, relevant to the person's ability to do the job – after a reasonable adjustment, if necessary.

An applicant with a visual impairment is asked at interview whether or not she was born with that condition. This is irrelevant to her ability to do the job and may upset the applicant, potentially preventing her from performing as well as she would otherwise have done. This is likely to be unlawful.

An applicant who is a wheelchair user is asked whether any changes may be needed to the workplace to accommodate him. This would not be unlawful.

7.28 Asking a basic question as to whether or not a person is disabled is unlikely to yield any useful information for the employer and may simply lead to confusion. The fact that such a question was asked might subsequently be used as evidence of discrimination. In addition, short-listing on the basis of an applicant's responses to a medical questionnaire may be discriminatory if the employer has not ascertained the likely effects of a disability or medical condition on the applicant's ability to do the job, or whether reasonable adjustments would overcome any disadvantage it causes. Even where there are medical requirements which must be met, it is good practice for employers not to require job applicants to answer a medical questionnaire until after a conditional job offer has been made.

7.29 On the other hand, when inviting a job applicant to attend an interview, it is good practice for an employer to ask whether any adjustments might be needed to enable him to participate fully in the process, and what those adjustments might be.

An application form includes the statement 'Please let us know if you require any reasonable adjustments, due to disability, to enable you to attend an interview, or which you wish us to take into account when considering your application. Reasonable adjustments are things like sign language interpreters, altering the time of the interview, or making the interview room accessible for you. If you would like to discuss your disability requirements further, please contact the Human Resources manager'. This will not be discriminatory and is likely to help an employer comply with its duties under the Act.

7.30 In addition, once a decision has been made to appoint a disabled person, it is good practice for an employer to discuss reasonable adjustments with him before he starts work. An employer may also wish to monitor disabled applicants, as part of an overall monitoring policy, although this information should be kept separately from an application form. More information about good practice in relation to monitoring is given in paragraphs 2.14 to 2.16.

Can a disabled person be required to have a medical examination?

7.31 Although the Act does not prevent an employer from asking a disabled person to have a medical examination, an employer will probably be discriminating unlawfully if, without justification, it insists on a medical check for a disabled person but not for others. The fact that a person has a disability is, in itself, unlikely to justify singling out that person to have a health check – although this might be justified in relation to some jobs. Paragraphs 6.14 to 6.16 explain the circumstances in which medical information may legitimately influence an employer's decision as to whether to offer a job to a disabled person.

> An employer requires all candidates for employment to have a medical examination. The employer would be entitled to apply that requirement to a disabled person who applies for employment.

> An employer issues a health questionnaire to all job applicants and requires any successful job applicant who states they are disabled to undergo a medical examination. This is likely to be unlawful.

> An employer issues a health questionnaire to all successful job applicants but does not require them to undergo a medical examination unless they have a condition which may be relevant to the job, or the working environment. A successful job applicant indicates that he has a disabling heart condition. It is likely that the employer would be justified in asking him to have a medical examination provided it is restricted to assessing the implications for the particular job in question.

Offers of employment

7.32 Terms and conditions of service should not discriminate against a disabled person. In general, an employer should not offer a job to a disabled person on terms which are less favourable than those which would be offered to other people.

A person with a history of depression is offered employment with a six month probationary period, even though other employees are only required to serve a three month probationary period. This will amount to direct discrimination and will be unlawful.

8 Discrimination against employees

Introduction

8.1 It has already been explained (at paragraph 3.19) that it is unlawful for an employer to discriminate against a disabled person whom it employs:

s 4(2)

- in the terms of employment which it affords him

- in the opportunities which it affords him for promotion, a transfer, training or receiving any other benefit

- by refusing to afford him, or deliberately not affording him, any such opportunity, or

- by dismissing him, or subjecting him to any other detriment.

8.2 This chapter examines these principles in more detail. In order to do so, it is necessary to look at various aspects of the employment relationship and its associated conditions and benefits, from terms and conditions of service to arrangements for induction and training, and from opportunities for promotion or transfer to arrangements for managing disability or ill health, and terminating employment.

8.3 Although the following paragraphs refer only to the treatment of employees, it should be remembered that the same principles apply to people in occupations covered by the Act's provisions on employment and occupation. Any variations in the way the Act applies to such occupations are explained in Chapter 9. In addition, particular issues about discrimination in providing occupational pensions and group insurance services are considered in Chapter 10.

Terms and conditions of service

8.4 As stated at paragraph 7.32, terms and conditions of service should not discriminate against a disabled person. The employer should consider whether any reasonable adjustments need to be made to the terms and conditions which would otherwise apply.

> An employer's terms and conditions state the hours an employee has to be in work. It might be a reasonable adjustment to change these hours for someone whose disability means that she has difficulty using public transport during rush hours.

8.5 Where the terms and conditions of employment include an element of performance-related pay, the employer must ensure that the way such pay arrangements operate does not discriminate against a disabled employee. If, on the ground of disability, an employee is denied the opportunity to receive performance-related pay, this is likely to be direct discrimination. Even if less favourable treatment of an employee in relation to performance-related pay is not directly discriminatory, it will amount to disability-related discrimination unless the employer can show that it is justified.

8.6 If an employee has a disability which adversely affects his rate of output, the effect may be that he receives less under a performance-related pay scheme than other employees. The employer must consider whether there are reasonable adjustments which would overcome this substantial disadvantage.

A disabled man with arthritis works in telephone sales and is paid commission on the value of his sales. Because of a worsening of his impairment he is advised to switch to new computer equipment. This equipment slows his work down for a period of time while he gets used to it and consequently the value of his sales falls. It is likely to be a reasonable adjustment for his employer to continue to pay him his previous level of commission for the period in which he adjusts to the new equipment.

A disabled home-worker, who is paid a fixed rate for each item he produces, has a reduced output rate because he does not have the right equipment to do the job to the best of his ability. It is likely to be a reasonable adjustment for the employer to provide that equipment, possibly with funding or advice from the Access to Work scheme, to improve the disabled worker's output and consequently his pay.

A woman who has recently become disabled because of diabetes works for an employer that operates a performance related bonus scheme. When she has her annual appraisal, the woman is unable to demonstrate that she has met all her objectives for the year, unlike in previous years when she had in fact exceeded her objectives. The reason why the woman has not met her objectives this year is that she has been adjusting to her disability (attending hospital appointments, paying careful attention to her diet, taking regular breaks etc.). The disabled woman's employer is likely to be discriminating against her if, because she has not met her objectives for the year, it refuses to pay her a bonus.

Induction, training and development

s 4(2) & s 4A(1)

8.7 Employers must not discriminate in their induction procedures. The employer may have to make adjustments to ensure a disabled person is introduced into a new working environment in a clearly structured and supported way, with an individually tailored induction programme if necessary.

A small manufacturing company usually hands out written copies of all its policies by way of induction to new employees and gives them half a day to read the documentation and to raise any questions with their line manager. A new employee has dyslexia and the employer arranges for her supervisor to spend a morning with her talking through the relevant policies. This is likely to be a reasonable adjustment.

An employer runs a one day induction course for new recruits. A recruit with a learning disability is put at a substantial disadvantage by the way the course is normally run. The employer is likely to have to make an alternative arrangement such as permitting the person to attend a longer course, or allowing someone to sit in on the course to provide support, assistance or encouragement to the disabled person.

8.8 In addition, employers must not discriminate in selection for training and must make reasonable adjustments in order to avoid disabled people being placed at a substantial disadvantage.

s 4(2) & s 4A(1)

> Instead of taking an informed decision, an employer wrongly assumes that a disabled person will be unwilling or unable to undertake demanding training or attend a residential training course. This is likely to amount to direct discrimination.

> An employer may need to alter the time or the location of the training for someone with a mobility problem, make training manuals, slides or other visual media accessible to a visually impaired employee (perhaps by providing Braille versions or having them read out), or ensure that an induction loop is available for someone with a hearing impairment.

> An employee with a hearing impairment is selected for a post as a TV engineer. He attends the induction course which consists of a video and discussion. The video is not subtitled and thus the employee cannot participate fully in the induction. This is likely to be unlawful.

> An employer refuses to allow a disabled employee to be coached for a theory examination relating to practical work which the employee is unable to do because of his disability. This is likely to be justified because the employee would never be suited for the area of work for which the coaching was designed, and a reasonable adjustment could not alter that position.

8

However, if the disabled employee required coaching to enable him to understand the requirements of the practical work because he would be managing staff carrying out the work, a decision not to provide coaching would be unlikely to be justified.

Benefits provided by employers

s 4(2) & s 4A(1)

8.9 Employers often provide a range of benefits to their staff. 'Benefits' include 'facilities' and 'services'. An employer must not discriminate in the way that it makes benefits available to disabled employees where those benefits are available to other employees. The employer must make any necessary reasonable adjustment to the way the benefits are provided. As explained in Chapter 10, an employer's duty to make reasonable adjustments now extends to the way it provides any benefits relating to occupational pension schemes or group insurance services.

8.10 Benefits might include canteens, meal vouchers, social clubs and other recreational activities, dedicated car parking spaces, discounts on products, bonuses, share options, hairdressing, clothes allowances, financial services, healthcare, medical assistance/insurance, transport to work, company car, education assistance, workplace nurseries, and rights to special leave. This is not an exhaustive list.

If physical features of a company's social club would inhibit a disabled person's access it might be a reasonable adjustment for the employer to make suitable modifications.

> An employer provides dedicated car parking spaces close to the workplace. A disabled employee finds it very difficult to get from the public car parks further away. It is likely to be a reasonable adjustment for the employer to allocate one of the dedicated spaces to that employee.

8.11 Some benefits may continue after employment has ended. An employer's duties under the Act extend to its former employees in respect of such benefits.

s 16A

8.12 The provisions on employment and occupation in Part 2 do not normally apply to benefits which an employer provides to the public, or to a section of the public which includes the disabled employee. This is because the provision of those benefits relates to the employer's activities as a service provider rather than as an employer. Such activities are usually subject to the duties in Part 3 instead. However, the Act's provisions on employment and occupation will apply if the benefit to employees is materially different (for example, at a discount) or is governed by the contract of employment, or relates to training.

s 4(2) & (4)

8

> A disabled employee of a supermarket chain is discriminated against for a reason related to his disability when buying goods as a customer of the supermarket. Even though he is an employee, he would have no claim under the Act's provisions on employment and occupation, because he is merely buying goods as a customer. However, if the discrimination related to the use of his employee's discount card, that would relate to his employment benefits and the Act's provisions on employment and occupation would apply.

Promotion and transfer

s 4(2) &
s 4A(1)

8.13 Employers must ensure that arrangements for promoting staff, or for transferring staff between jobs, do not discriminate against disabled people. It is likely to be direct discrimination if a disabled employee is treated less favourably in this regard on the ground of disability (see paragraph 4.5). If the treatment is not directly discriminatory, but is for a reason related to the disability, it will amount to disability-related discrimination unless the employer can show that it is justified. Employers must not discriminate in the practical arrangements necessary to enable the promotion or transfer to take place or, of course, in the new job itself. Reasonable adjustments may need to be made to the various stages in the promotion or transfer process.

> A garage owner does not consider a clerk, who has lost the use of her right arm, for promotion to assistant manager because he wrongly and unreasonably believes that her disability might prevent her performing competently in a managerial post. This is likely to be discrimination.

> An employer interviewing a number of people for promotion is aware that one of the candidates has a hearing impairment, but does not find out whether he needs any special arrangements. The candidate requires a sign language interpreter. It is likely to be a reasonable adjustment to arrange for an interpreter.

8

A woman who has a disability resulting from a back injury is seeking a transfer to a different department. A minor aspect of the role she seeks involves assisting with unloading the weekly delivery van – but she is unable to do this because of her disability. In assessing her suitability for transfer, the employer should consider whether reallocating this duty to someone else would be a reasonable step to take.

A disabled teacher who has depression applies for a promotion to be a Head of Department in her school. The Head Teacher responsible for filling this post says that the woman would be unsuitable because she would not be able to cope with the stress of the job. He has no evidence that this would be the case, and is merely making an assumption about her disability. This is likely to be unlawful.

8.14 As with other aspects of employment, employers will be better placed to ensure that promotion and transfer arrangements do not discriminate against disabled people if they have established and implemented policies and practices to counter discrimination generally (see paragraph 2.12). These will help employers to check, for example, that qualifications required for promotion or transfer are justified for the job to be done, and to monitor other arrangements – such as systems for determining criteria for a particular job – so that they do not exclude disabled people who may have been unable to meet those criteria because of their disability but who would be capable of performing well in the job.

Managing disability or ill health

Retention of disabled employees

s 4(2)

8.15 An employer must not discriminate against an employee who becomes disabled, or who has a disability which worsens. Employers will often find that it is of benefit to their organisation to retain a disabled employee as this will prevent their knowledge and skills from being lost to the enterprise. In addition, the cost of retaining such an employee will frequently be less than the cost of recruiting and training a new member of staff.

8.16 If as a result of the disability an employer's arrangements or a physical feature of the employer's premises place the employee at a substantial disadvantage in doing his existing job, the employer must consider any reasonable adjustment that would resolve the difficulty. The nature of the adjustments which an employer may have to consider will depend on the circumstances of the case, but the following considerations will always be relevant:

- The first consideration in making reasonable adjustments should be to enable the disabled employee to continue in his present job if at all possible.

- The employer should consult the disabled person at appropriate stages about what his needs are and, where the employee has a progressive condition, what effect the disability might have on future employment, so that reasonable adjustments may be planned.

- In appropriate cases, the employer should also consider seeking expert advice on the extent of a disabled person's capabilities and on what might be done to change premises or working arrangements. Where an employee has been off work, a phased return might be appropriate.

■ If there are no reasonable adjustments which would enable the disabled employee to continue in his present job, the employer must consider whether there are suitable alternative positions to which he could be redeployed.

A nurse becomes disabled after a back injury. After talking to her and taking specialist advice, the employer decides that there are no reasonable adjustments that could be made to her present role. The employer then considers whether there is another role that would be suitable and offers an alternative post to the employee, at roughly the same level of seniority. However, if after considering these steps, it is apparent that there is no alternative position on a similar salary and with similar conditions, a position on a lower salary or with worse conditions could be offered as a reasonable adjustment.

8.17 It may be possible to modify a job to accommodate an employee's changing needs. This might be by rearranging working methods or giving another employee certain minor tasks that the disabled person can no longer do, or by providing practical aids or adaptations to premises or equipment, or allowing the disabled person to work at different times or places from those with equivalent jobs. It may be that a reduction in working hours is appropriate.

8

A newly disabled employee may need time to readjust. In those circumstances, an employer might allow a trial period to assess whether the employee is able to cope with the current job, with or without modifications; the employee may initially be permitted to work from home, or with a gradual build-up to full time hours.

It may be a reasonable adjustment for an employer to move a newly disabled person to a different post within the organisation if a suitable vacancy exists or is expected shortly.

Additional job coaching may be necessary to enable a disabled person to take on a new job.

8.18 The issue of job retention might also arise when an employee has a stable impairment but the nature of his job changes. In these circumstances an employer may also have a duty to make reasonable adjustments.

A woman with a learning disability is allocated to a new department because of a business reorganisation. She is given extra training to enable her to carry out her new role. This is likely to be a reasonable adjustment for the employer to make.

An employer installs a new software system for all computer users in the office. A disabled man who uses voice-activated software finds that this software is not compatible with the new office computer software. The employer provides him with new voice-activated software which is compatible with the office system. It also offers him appropriate training in the use of the two new software systems. These are likely to be reasonable adjustments for the employer to make.

Access to Work Scheme

8.19 In determining what adjustments to make to facilitate the employment of a disabled person, employers should have regard to the range of advice and assistance which is available from Jobcentre Plus through the Access to Work scheme. The purpose of the scheme is to provide practical support to disabled people in, or entering, paid employment to help overcome work related obstacles resulting from disability. Access to Work provides a grant towards these additional employment costs. However, there is no automatic right to support from the Access to Work scheme – this is subject to an assessment when an application for support is made by the disabled person.

8.20 The Access to Work scheme may assist an employer to decide what steps to take. If financial assistance is available from the scheme, it may also make it reasonable for an employer to take certain steps which would otherwise be unreasonably expensive. However, Access to Work does not diminish any of an employer's duties under the Act. In particular:

■ the responsibility for making a reasonable adjustment is the responsibility of the employer – even where Access to Work is involved in the provision of advice or funding in relation to the adjustment

- it is likely to be a reasonable step for the employer to assist a disabled person in making an application for assistance from Access to Work and to provide ongoing administrative support (by completing claim forms, for example), and

- it may be unreasonable for an employer to decide not to make an adjustment if the decision is based on the cost of the adjustment but before it is known if financial assistance for it is available from Access to Work or another source.

Further information about what the Access to Work scheme can offer, the scheme's eligibility requirements, and how to apply, is set out in Appendix C.

Confidential information

8.21 The extent to which an employer is entitled to let other staff know about an employee's disability will depend partly on the terms of employment. An employer could be discriminating against the employee by revealing such information if the employer would not reveal similar information about another person for an equally legitimate management purpose; or if the employer revealed such information without consulting the individual, instead of adopting the usual practice of talking to an employee before revealing personal information about him. Employers also need to be aware that they have obligations under the Data Protection Act in respect of personal data.

8.22 However, as noted at paragraph 5.22, sometimes a reasonable adjustment will not work without the co-operation of other employees. In order to secure such co-operation, it may be necessary for the employer to tell one or more of a disabled person's colleagues (in confidence) about a disability which is not obvious. This may be limited to the disabled person's supervisor, or it may be appropriate to involve other colleagues, depending on the nature of the disability and the reason they need to know about it. In any event, an employer must not disclose confidential details about an employee without his consent. A disabled person's refusal to give such consent may impact upon the effectiveness of the adjustments which the employer is able to make or its ability to make adjustments at all.

> In order for a person with epilepsy to work safely in a particular factory, it may be necessary to advise fellow workers about how they can assist the disabled worker to manage her condition.

> An office worker with cancer says that he does not want colleagues to know of his condition. As an adjustment he needs extra time away from work to receive treatment and to rest. Neither his colleagues nor the line manager need to be told the precise reasons for the extra leave but the latter will need to know that the adjustment is required in order to implement it effectively.

8.23 The Act does not prevent a disabled person keeping a disability confidential from an employer. But keeping a disability confidential is likely to mean that unless the employer could reasonably be expected to know about it anyway, the employer will not be under a duty to make a reasonable adjustment. If a disabled person expects an employer to make a reasonable adjustment, he will need to provide the employer – or someone acting on its behalf - with sufficient information to carry out that adjustment.

An employee has symptomatic HIV. He prefers not to tell his employer of the condition. However, as the condition progresses, he finds it increasingly difficult to work the required number of hours in a week. Until he tells his employer of his condition – or the employer becomes aware of it (or could reasonably be expected to be aware of it) – the employer does not have to make a reasonable adjustment by changing his working hours to overcome the difficulty. However, once the employer is informed he may then have to make a reasonable adjustment.

Termination of employment

8.24 Where a disabled person is dismissed or is selected for redundancy or for compulsory early retirement (including compulsory ill-health retirement), the employer must ensure that the disabled person is not being discriminated against. It is likely to be direct discrimination if the dismissal or selection is made on the ground of disability (see paragraph 4.5). If the dismissal or selection is not directly discriminatory, but is made for a reason related to the disability, it will amount to disability-related discrimination unless the employer can show that it is justified. The reason would also have to be one which could not be removed by any reasonable adjustment.

It would be justifiable to terminate the employment of an employee whose disability makes it impossible for him to perform the main functions of his job any longer, if an adjustment such as a move to a vacant post elsewhere in the business is not practicable or otherwise not reasonable for the employer to have to make.

8.25 When setting criteria for redundancy selection, employers should consider whether any proposed criterion would adversely impact upon a disabled employee. If so, it may be necessary for the employer to make reasonable adjustments. For example, it is likely to be a reasonable adjustment to discount disability-related sickness absence when assessing attendance as part of a redundancy selection scheme. Some employers use 'flexibility' as a selection criterion for redundancy (for example, willingness to re-locate or to work unpopular hours, or ability to carry out a wide variety of tasks). An employer should carefully consider how to apply this criterion to a disabled employee as it might be discriminatory.

8.26 Where the dismissal of a disabled person is being considered for a reason relating to that person's conduct, the employer should consider whether any reasonable adjustments need to be made to the disciplinary or dismissal process. In addition, if the conduct in question is related to the employee's disability, that may be relevant in determining the sanction which it is appropriate to impose.

A young man with learning disabilities asks if he can bring a friend to a disciplinary hearing, rather than a work colleague. It is likely to be a reasonable adjustment for his employer to allow this.

8

> A woman shouts at her line manager in front of work colleagues and uses inappropriate language. The employer would usually consider dismissal as a sanction for such behaviour, but takes into account the fact that she was in great pain on the day in question because of her disability and instead issues a warning. This is likely to be a reasonable adjustment to make.

s 4(5) 8.27 A disabled person will be taken to have been dismissed for the purposes of the Act if:

- he is expressly dismissed, or

- the period for which he is employed expires without his employment being immediately renewed on the same terms, or

- he gives notice, or does some other act to bring his employment to an end in circumstances in which he is entitled to terminate it without notice by reason of the employer's conduct (this is known as 'constructive dismissal').

After the termination of employment

s 16A(3) 8.28 Where a disabled person's employment has come to an end, the Act says that it will still be unlawful for his former employer:

- to discriminate against him by subjecting him to a detriment, or

- to subject him to harassment

if the discrimination or harassment arises out of the employment which has come to an end and is closely connected to it.

> A disabled person working as a sales consultant has to go back to his former workplace for a meeting to finalise handover of his customer files to his replacement. On arrival, he is verbally abused by one of his former colleagues. The abuse relates to his disability. This is unlawful.

8.29 It is also unlawful to victimise a person (whether or not he is disabled) after his employment has come to an end (see paragraphs 4.33 to 4.36).

s 55

> A disabled person gives the name of his former employer as a referee for a new job. The employer gives him a poor reference, referring to his disability as being a hindrance. This poor reference is an untrue reflection of the standard of work carried out by the disabled person. The poor reference was given because he brought a claim of disability discrimination against his former employer. Consequently it is unlawful.

8

8.30 An employer's duty to make reasonable adjustments may also apply in respect of a former employee who is a disabled person. This will be the case where:

s 16A(4) - (6)

- the disabled person is placed at a substantial disadvantage in comparison with other former employees:

   a. by a provision, practice or criterion applied by the employer to the disabled person in relation to any matter arising out of his former employment, or

   b. by a physical feature of premises occupied by the employer, and

- the employer either knows, or could reasonably be expected to know, that the former employee in question has a disability and is likely to be affected in this way.

> A former employee with life-time membership of the works social club is no longer able to access the club because of a mobility impairment. Once the employer becomes aware of the problem, it will need to consider making reasonable adjustments.

8.31 The former employees with whom the position of the disabled person should be compared must be people who are not disabled, but who are former employees of the same employer. If it is not possible to identify an actual comparator for this purpose, then a hypothetical comparator may be used (see paragraph 4.18).

8.32 The principles relating to post-termination discrimination also apply to other relationships covered by Part 2, and to the relationship between a provider of employment services and its former clients. These relationships are considered in the following chapters.

Discrimination in occupation

Introduction

9.1 The preceding chapters focus on discrimination against employees. However, as noted at paragraph 3.11, Part 2 of the Act also applies to certain occupations. This chapter explains the relevant provisions.

9.2 The following paragraphs explain the provisions of Part 2 which focus specifically on the occupations in question. In other respects, however, the employment provisions of the Act apply in the usual way. So, where appropriate, regard should be had to the matters concerning recruitment and retention which are explained in Chapters 7 and 8; occupational pension schemes and group insurance services (Chapter 10); adjustments to premises (Chapter 12); and to the other relevant issues (Chapter 13).

Discrimination against contract workers

What does the Act say about contract workers?

9.3 The Act says that it is unlawful for a 'principal' to discriminate against a disabled contract worker:

s 4B(1)

- in the terms on which he is allowed to do 'contract work'

- by not allowing him to do, or continue to do, contract work

- in the way it affords him access to, or by failing to afford him access to, benefits in relation to contract work, or

- by subjecting him to any other detriment.

s 4B(2)
s 55

9.4 The Act also says that it is unlawful for a principal to subject a disabled contract worker to harassment or to victimise any contract worker, whether or not he is disabled.

s 4B(9)

9.5 For this purpose, 'contract work' is work which an individual carries out for a person (a 'principal') who hires him under a contract made with his employer. Usually, that contract is made directly between the principal and the contract worker's employer, (which is generally an employment business), but this is not always the case. Provided that there is an unbroken chain of contracts between the individual and the end-user of his services, that end-user is a principal for the purposes of the Act, and so the individual is a contract worker.

A disabled person works for a computer software company which sometimes uses an employment business to deploy staff to work on projects for other companies. The employment business arranges for the disabled person to work on a project for a large supermarket chain. In this case the 'principal' is the supermarket chain.

9.6 The effect of the Act is that, where a person is a principal for the purposes of the Act, he is treated as if he were, or would be, the actual employer of the disabled contract worker. Therefore, the same principles relating to discrimination apply to a principal as to an employer.

> The employer of a labourer, who some years ago was disabled by clinical depression but has since recovered, proposes to supply him to a contractor to work on a building site. Although his past disability is covered by the Act, the contractor's site manager refuses to accept him because of his medical history. The contractor is likely to be acting unlawfully.

How does the duty to make reasonable adjustments apply in respect of disabled contract workers?

9.7 The duty to make reasonable adjustments applies to a principal in the same way as it applies to an employer.

s 4B(6)

9.8 However, in deciding whether any, and if so, what, adjustments would be reasonable for a principal to make, the period for which the disabled contract worker will work for the principal is important. It might well be unreasonable for a principal to have to make certain adjustments if the worker will be with the principal for only a short time.

> An employment business enters into a contract with a firm of accountants to provide an assistant for two weeks to cover an unexpected absence. The employment business proposes a name. The person concerned finds it difficult, because of his disability, to travel during the rush hour and would like his working hours to be modified accordingly. It might not be reasonable for the firm to have to agree, given the short time in which to negotiate and implement the new hours.

9

9.9 In the case of a disabled contract worker, both his employer and the principal to whom he is supplied may separately be under a duty to make reasonable adjustments.

> A travel agency hires a clerical worker from an employment business to fulfil a three month contract to file travel invoices during the busy summer holiday period. The contract worker is a wheelchair user, and is quite capable of doing the job if a few minor, temporary changes are made to the arrangement of furniture in the office. It is likely to be reasonable for the travel agency to make these adjustments.

s 4A(1)

9.10 A disabled contract worker's employer will have to make reasonable adjustments if the contract worker is substantially disadvantaged by the employer's own premises – or by a provision, criterion or practice applied by it. The Act says **s 4B(4) & (5)** that the employer will also have to make reasonable adjustments where the contract worker is likely to be substantially disadvantaged by the premises – or by a provision criterion or practice – of all or most of the principals to whom he might be supplied. This duty only arises if the contract worker is likely to be affected in this way each time he is supplied for work. The employer would have to make reasonable adjustments to overcome the disadvantage wherever it might arise, rather than taking separate steps in relation to each principal.

> A blind secretary is employed by an employment business which supplies her to other organisations for secretarial work. Her ability to access standard computer equipment places her at a substantial disadvantage at the offices of all or most of the principals to whom she might be supplied. The employment business provides her with a specially adapted portable computer and Braille keyboard.

9.11 A principal has the same duties to make reasonable adjustments as a disabled contract worker's employer, but does not have to make any adjustment which the employer should make. So, in effect, the principal is responsible for any additional reasonable adjustments which are necessary solely because of its own arrangements or premises.

s 4A(1) applied by s 4B(6) & (7)

> In the preceding example, a bank which hired the blind secretary may have to make changes which are necessary to ensure that the computer provided by the employment business is compatible with the system which the bank is already using.

9.12 It would be reasonable for a principal and the employer of a contract worker to co-operate with any steps taken by the other to assist the contract worker. It is good practice for the principal and the employer to discuss what adjustments should be made – and who should make them.

> The bank and the employment business in the preceding examples would need to co-operate with each other so that, for example, the

9

employment business allows the bank to make any necessary adaptations to the equipment which the employment business provided to ensure its compatibility with the bank's existing systems.

What about Workstep?

9.13 These arrangements also apply to the Workstep scheme (formerly known as the Supported Placement Scheme) operated by Jobcentre Plus for severely disabled people. The 'contractor' under the scheme (usually a local authority or voluntary body) is the equivalent of the contract worker's own employer, and the 'host employer' is the equivalent of the principal. A local authority can even be both the contractor and the host employer at the same time (as can a voluntary body).

Discrimination against office holders

Who are office holders?

s 4C

9.14 Examples of office holders include some company directors, judges, and chairmen or members of non-departmental public bodies. What the holders of such offices or posts have in common is that they are not regarded as 'employees' by the law, even though they may be similar to employees in providing services personally under the direction of another in return for remuneration. The Act gives specific protection to such office holders against discrimination if they are not otherwise protected under Part 2. This protection extends to applicants for such appointments and applies also to office holders appointed by, or on the recommendation of, the Government (including the devolved administrations for Scotland and Wales), or subject to its approval. However, it does not extend to the holders of political office.

9.15 The Act says that, in relation to an appointment to such an office or post, it is unlawful to discriminate against a disabled person: **s 4D(1)**

- in the arrangements which are made to determine who should be offered the appointment

- in the terms on which the appointment is offered, or

- by refusing to offer him the appointment.

9.16 In addition, where the appointment is made on the Government's recommendation (or is subject to its approval) the Act says that it is unlawful to discriminate against a disabled person: **s 4D(2)**

- in the arrangements which are made to determine who should be recommended or approved, or

- in making or refusing to make a recommendation, or in giving or refusing to give approval.

> A deaf woman who communicates using British Sign Language applies for appointment as a member of a public body. Without interviewing her, the public body making the appointments writes to her saying that she would not be suitable as good communication skills are a requirement. This is likely to be unlawful.

9.17 The Act also says that it is unlawful, in relation to a disabled person who has been appointed to such an office or post, to discriminate against him: **s 4D(3)**

9

- in the terms of the appointment

- in the opportunities which are afforded (or refused) for promotion, a transfer, training or receiving any other benefit

- by terminating the appointment, or

- by subjecting him to any other detriment in relation to the appointment.

s 4D(4)
s 55

9.18 In addition, the Act says that it is unlawful to subject a disabled person to harassment if he is an office holder, or if he is seeking or being considered for an appointment (or a related Government recommendation or approval). It is also unlawful to victimise such a person, whether he is disabled or not.

s 4D(5)

9.19 As far as benefits are concerned, the Act mirrors the position in respect of benefits to employees (see paragraphs 8.9 to 8.12).

s 16B

9.20 The Act gives the DRC power to take action in respect of a discriminatory advertisement for appointment to an office or post (see paragraphs 13.28 to 13.30). This mirrors the DRC's power in respect of advertisements for employment (see paragraphs 7.12 and 7.13).

How does the duty to make reasonable adjustments apply in respect of office holders?

s 4E(1)

9.21 Part 2 also requires reasonable adjustments to be made for disabled people holding relevant offices or posts, or seeking such appointments. The duty relates to any provision, criterion or practice applied by or on behalf of the relevant person (see paragraph 9.22), and to any physical feature of premises under the control of such a person where the functions of the office or post are performed.

A selection process is carried out to appoint the chair of a public health body. The best candidate is found to be a disabled person with a progressive condition who is not able to work full-time because of her disability. Whoever makes or recommends the appointment should consider whether it would be a reasonable adjustment to appoint the disabled person on a job-share or part-time basis.

Who needs to avoid discriminating against office holders?

9.22 The effect of the Act is to give a disabled person holding a relevant office or post, or seeking or being considered for appointment, similar rights to those of an employee or job applicant. In the employment context, it is clearly the employer who has the obligations under the Act. However, in relation to office holders, the person on whom the duties are imposed ('the relevant person') depends on the circumstances. It may be:

s 4F(2)

- the person with power to make the appointment

- the person or body with power to recommend or approve the appointment

- the person with power to determine the terms or working conditions of the appointment (including any benefit or physical feature), or

- the person with power to terminate the appointment.

Discrimination against police officers

9.23 Not all police officers are regarded as 'employees' in law. However, the Act says that all police officers and police cadets count as employees for

s 64A

the purposes of Part 2. As a result, disabled police officers and police cadets (and disabled people applying to join the police service) have the same rights as other employees and job applicants under Part 2. These include rights in respect of harassment and victimisation (the latter extending to non-disabled people as well as to those who are disabled).

9.24 These rights – which also apply in respect of special constables and small police forces such as the British Transport Police – are enforceable against the relevant chief officer of police or police authority (or the relevant chief constable in the case of Scottish police forces). In addition, a chief officer of police (or chief constable) is liable under the Act for the discriminatory acts of one police officer (or cadet) committed against another.

Discrimination against partners in firms

What does the Act say about partners in firms?

s 6A(1) 9.25 The Act says that it is unlawful for a firm, in relation to a position as a partner in the firm, to discriminate against a disabled person:

- in the arrangements it makes to determine who should be offered that position

- in the terms on which it offers him that position

- by refusing or deliberately omitting to offer him that position, or

- where the disabled person is already a partner in the firm:

   a. in the way it affords him access to any benefits, or by refusing or deliberately omitting to afford him access to them, or

b. by expelling him from the partnership, or subjecting him to any other detriment.

9.26 The Act also says that it is unlawful for a firm to subject a disabled person who is an existing or prospective partner to harassment, or to victimise any existing or prospective partner, whether or not he is disabled.

s 6A(2)
s 55

9.27 The effect of the Act is to give a partner or applicant for partnership similar rights against the firm to those of an employee or job applicant against an employer. The same applies where people are proposing to form themselves into a partnership and a disabled person is a prospective partner. Limited liability partnerships are also covered.

s 6C

A group of self-employed accountants decide to go into partnership. One of them discloses that he is disabled because of cancer. The others decide to go ahead and form a partnership without the disabled person because they are worried about him being absent from work for medical treatment. This is likely to be unlawful.

9.28 As far as benefits are concerned, (and in common with the rules which apply to office holders), the Act mirrors the position in respect of benefits to employees (see paragraphs 8.9 to 8.12).

s 6A(3)

9.29 The Act gives the DRC power to take action in respect of a discriminatory advertisement for any partnership in a firm (see paragraphs 13.28 to 13.30). This mirrors the DRC's power in respect of advertisements for employment (see paragraphs 7.12 and 7.13).

s 16B

s 6B(1)

9.30 The duty to make reasonable adjustments applies to a firm in the same way as it applies to an employer. It relates to any provision, criterion or practice applied by or on behalf of the firm and to any physical feature of premises occupied by the firm.

s 6B(4)

9.31 Although, in general, the cost of making a reasonable adjustment cannot be passed on to the disabled person concerned, where a firm is required to make adjustments in respect of a disabled partner or prospective partner, the cost of doing so is an expense of the firm. Provided that the disabled person is, or becomes, a partner in the firm, he may be required to make a reasonable contribution towards this expense. In assessing the reasonableness of any such contribution, particular regard should be had to the proportion in which the disabled partner is entitled to share in the firm's profits.

> A disabled person who uses a wheelchair as a result of a mobility impairment joins a firm of architects as a partner, receiving 20% of the firm's profits. He is asked to pay 20% towards the cost of a lift which must be installed so that he can work on the premises. This is likely to be reasonable.

Discrimination against barristers and advocates

s 7A(1)

9.32 The Act says that, in England and Wales, it is unlawful for a barrister or a barrister's clerk, in relation to any offer of a pupillage or tenancy, to discriminate against a disabled person:

- in the arrangements which are made to determine to whom it should be offered

- in respect of any terms on which it is offered, or

- by refusing or deliberately omitting to offer it to him.

9.33 The Act also says that it is unlawful for a barrister or barrister's clerk, in relation to a disabled pupil or tenant in the set of chambers in question, to discriminate against him:

s 7A(2)

- in respect of any terms applicable to him as a pupil or tenant

- in the opportunities for training, or gaining experience, which are afforded or denied to him

- in the benefits which are afforded or denied to him

- by terminating his pupillage or by subjecting him to any pressure to leave the chambers, or

- by subjecting him to any other detriment.

> A solicitor telephones chambers to instruct a particular barrister, who is disabled, to appear in a particular Crown Court case. The clerk assumes that the court is not accessible and passes the brief to another barrister. This is likely to be unlawful.

9.34 In addition, the Act says that it is unlawful for a barrister or barrister's clerk to subject a disabled person who is a pupil or tenant in a set of

s 7A(3)
s 55

chambers (or who has applied to be a pupil or tenant) to harassment, or to victimise such a person, whether he is disabled or not. In effect, therefore, barristers and pupils have rights under Part 2 which are similar to the rights of employees.

s 7A(5)

9.35 Barristers who are permitted to practise from a set of chambers, but who are not tenants (barristers who do this are colloquially known as 'squatters'), have the same rights under Part 2 as barristers who are tenants.

s 7C
s 55

9.36 In Scotland, advocates do not practise in sets of chambers. However, the Act makes it unlawful for a Scottish advocate to discriminate against a disabled pupil or to subject him to harassment. It is also unlawful to victimise a pupil, whether or not he is disabled. Disabled pupils (and prospective pupils) in Scotland have rights under Part 2 which are equivalent to those of their counterparts in England and Wales.

s 7A(4) &
s 7C(4)

9.37 The Act also says that it is unlawful to discriminate against a disabled person in relation to the giving, withholding or acceptance of instructions to a barrister or an advocate. It would therefore be unlawful for a solicitor to refuse to instruct a barrister or an advocate merely because they have a disability.

s 16B

9.38 The Act gives the DRC power to take action in respect of a discriminatory advertisement for any tenancy or pupillage (see paragraphs 13.28 to 13.30). This mirrors the DRC's power in respect of advertisements for employment (see paragraphs 7.12 and 7.13).

9.39 In England and Wales, the duty to make reasonable adjustments applies to barristers and barrister's clerks in the same way as it applies to an employer. It relates to any provision, criterion or practice applied by or on behalf of a barrister or barrister's clerk and to any physical feature of premises occupied by a barrister or by a barrister's clerk. Nevertheless, although it is unlawful to discriminate against a disabled barrister or pupil in relation to the giving, withholding or acceptance of instructions, it should be noted that a solicitor is under no duty to make a reasonable adjustment in relation to a disabled barrister whom he instructs.

s 7B(1)

9.40 Where a group of barristers practise together in a set of chambers, the duty to make reasonable adjustments applies to each individual barrister who has responsibility for any disadvantage to the disabled person if the adjustment is not made. Chambers need to consider whether their practices could disadvantage disabled pupils and tenant barristers. For example, the practice of writing messages on scrap paper is likely to disadvantage visually impaired members of chambers, and may need to be altered for individual disabled tenants and pupils.

s 7B(2)

9

9.41 The application of the duty to Scottish advocates is slightly more restricted, in recognition of the fact that Scottish advocates do not practise in sets of chambers, but tend to practise from home. Disabled pupils (and prospective pupils) in Scotland do have rights in respect of reasonable adjustments which are equivalent to those of their counterparts in England and Wales. However,

s 7D

where a disabled pupil is engaged by an advocate who practises from home, that may affect the extent of the adjustments which it is reasonable for the advocate to make (see paragraph 5.41).

Discrimination in relation to practical work experience

What does the Act say about practical work experience?

s 14C(1)

9.42 The Act says that it is unlawful for a 'placement provider' to discriminate against a disabled person who is seeking or undertaking a work placement:

- in the arrangements he makes for determining who should be offered a work placement

- in the terms on which he affords him access to any work placement or any facilities concerned with such placement

A bank offers three month placements in its accounts department to students on a business studies course. A disabled student is offered a placement on the basis that it lasts for only two weeks as it is believed – without asking the student herself – that she will not be able to cope with a three month placement. This is likely to be unlawful.

- by refusing or deliberately omitting to afford him such access

A student with ME is refused a work placement at a primary school, as it is believed that she will not be 'up to the job' because of her disability. This is likely to be unlawful.

- by terminating his placement

> A person with a mental health problem on a four week placement has to take a morning off to attend a hospital appointment related to her disability. The placement is terminated as a result of this. This is likely to be unlawful.

- by subjecting him to any other detriment during the placement

> A design company offers work placements in its creative department. People on placement do a range of things, including research and design. A person with a hearing impairment is given only photocopying to do on his placement because the supervisor does not think that he can do anything else. This would be subjecting the disabled person to a detriment and is likely to be unlawful.

9.43 The Act also says that it is unlawful for a placement provider to subject a disabled person to harassment if he is providing a work placement to that person, or if that person has applied to him for a work placement, or to victimise such a person, whether he is disabled or not.

s 14C(2)
s 55

> An employee at a company gives evidence in a tribunal case on behalf of a disabled person who was refused a work placement because of his disability and who has brought a claim of discrimination. The employee is dismissed because of this. This is likely to be unlawful.

9

s 14C(4)

9.44 For these purposes, a work placement is practical work experience undertaken for a limited period for the purposes of a person's vocational training. A placement provider is any person who provides a work placement to a person whom he does not employ.

s 14C(3)

9.45 The above applies only to the extent that discrimination in relation to practical work experience is not the subject of other provisions of the Act, such as those relating to discrimination in the provision of goods, facilities and services, or to discrimination in education. The DRC has issued separate codes of practice giving guidance on the operation of Part 3 and Part 4 of the Act (see Appendix C for details).

> A university arranges work placements in industry for its students. The placement provider in this case is the company offering the work experience and is covered by the provisions of Part 2. The university itself is not covered by these provisions, but is instead subject to the provisions on education in Part 4.

> A sixth form college offers work placements for trainee teachers. In this case the college is a placement provider and is covered by the provisions of Part 2.

s 16B

9.46 The Act gives the DRC power to take action in respect of a discriminatory advertisement for any work placement (see paragraphs 13.28 to 13.30). This mirrors the DRC's powers in respect of advertisements for employment (see paragraphs 7.12 and 7.13).

9

9.47 The duty to make reasonable adjustments applies to a placement provider in the same way as it applies to an employer. The duty applies in respect of any provision, criterion or practice applied by or on behalf of the placement provider and to any physical feature of premises occupied by the provider.

s 14D

> A disabled person who has a heart condition obtains a six week placement at a computer company. Such placements are normally offered only on a full-time basis. However, because this would be too tiring for the disabled person, the placement provider allows him to work mornings only.

> A disabled student needs to be accompanied by her support worker whilst on work placement. The placement provider facilitates this by providing an additional work station for the support worker.

> While on a work placement, a student with learning disabilities is given personal instruction in health and safety procedures in the workplace, rather than written information.

9.48 The considerations outlined in Chapter 5 apply in determining what adjustments it is reasonable for a placement provider to make. However, the length of the placement will also be a relevant factor. Although many adjustments cost little or nothing to make, it is unlikely to be reasonable for

9

a placement provider to spend significant sums on individually-tailored adjustments in respect of short placements. Nevertheless, some disabled students undertaking work placements may be able to fund adjustments out of their Disabled Students Allowance. Alternatively, some disabled people may already have equipment which they are prepared to use in the workplace. In that case, the placement provider may have to make reasonable adjustments in order to facilitate the use of that equipment (for example, by ensuring that it is transported and stored safely, and is adequately insured whilst at the workplace).

> A person with a hearing impairment on a business studies course has a six week placement with a bank. As he requires an induction loop to participate in meetings, the bank obtains a temporary induction loop as a reasonable adjustment.

> A disabled person who uses voice activated software is assisted by the placement provider's IT department to install her own software onto a workplace computer. She is also provided with a headset and microphone to use with it.

> A placement provider arranges to transport a disabled person's ergonomic chair to the workplace so that she can use it during a three week work placement.

9.49 An organisation which sends a disabled person on a work placement may also have a duty under the Act to make reasonable adjustments in respect of that person.

> Where a course provider supplies a laptop computer for a visually impaired person to complete work, it would also be reasonable for it to supply the computer for that person to use during a related work placement.

9.50 It would be reasonable to expect the sending organisation and the placement provider to co-operate to ensure that appropriate adjustments are identified and made. It is good practice for a placement provider to ask a disabled person about reasonable adjustments before the placement begins, and to allow him to visit the workplace in advance to see how his needs can be addressed. Once a particular adjustment has been identified, it would be reasonable for the sending organisation and the placement provider to discuss its implementation in the light of their respective obligations under the Act.

Introduction

10.1 Chapter 8 explains how the Act protects disabled people from discrimination in employment. In particular, paragraph 8.9 makes the point that employers must not discriminate in the way that they make benefits available to disabled employees where those benefits are available to other employees. Some of the most significant benefits which employers commonly make available to their employees relate to occupational pensions and group insurance schemes. This chapter explains what the Act says about discrimination in providing these particular types of benefit. This includes discrimination by the employer and by others concerned with providing the benefit in question.

Occupational pension schemes

What does the Act say about employers?

10.2 As far as employers are concerned, Part 2 does not distinguish between discrimination in providing pensions and discrimination in relation to other benefits. This is subject to one qualification (explained at paragraphs 10.13 and 10.14) concerning the remedies available for discrimination under Part 2.

10.3 Thus, an employer must not discriminate against a disabled person in the opportunities it affords him for receiving pension benefits, or by refusing him, or deliberately not affording him, any such

s 4(2)
s 4A(1)

opportunity. The duty to make reasonable adjustments applies to the manner in which employers make pensions available to a disabled employee.

10.4 To the extent that an employer has control over matters relating to pension benefits afforded to employees, the usual principles about discrimination will apply under Part 2. As explained in Chapter 4, less favourable treatment of a disabled person in relation to such benefits may amount to direct discrimination or to disability-related discrimination. Discrimination may also occur because of a failure to comply with a duty to make a reasonable adjustment to any provision, criterion or practice in relation to pension benefits in respect of a disabled person.

A person with MS completes the first six months of her employment. After this period the employer usually writes to employees inviting them to join the pension scheme. The employer is worried, however, that the disabled employee may draw early on the pension scheme and so does not invite her to join. This is likely to be unlawful.

10.5 In relation to a well established pension scheme, the application of provisions, criteria and practices relating to pension benefits is likely to be controlled by the trustees or managers of the pension scheme. However, when new schemes are set up, employers are likely to have substantial input in relation to such matters (for example, setting scheme rules), and in doing so they must not discriminate against disabled people.

10

10.6 Part 2 contains provisions which relate specifically to discrimination against disabled people by the trustees or managers of occupational pension schemes. The principal effect of these provisions is to make it unlawful for pension scheme trustees or managers to contravene a 'non-discrimination rule' which is deemed to be included in every occupational pension scheme.

s 4G(3)

10.7 This non-discrimination rule effectively makes the trustees and managers of the scheme subject to the general provisions of Part 2 by doing two things:

■ First, the non-discrimination rule prohibits pension scheme trustees or managers from discriminating against a disabled person who is a member or prospective member of the scheme in carrying out any of their functions in relation to the scheme. This includes functions relating to the admission and treatment of members of the scheme.

s 4G(1)

■ Second, the rule prohibits the trustees or managers from subjecting such a person to harassment in relation to the scheme.

The Act sets out the circumstances in which a person counts as a prospective member of a pension scheme.

s 4K(2)

10

A disabled person applies to join an occupational pension scheme. The trustees say that he can join but as he has diabetes, he will not be able to take early retirement on health grounds. This decision is reached with no consideration of the individual circumstances and is likely to be unlawful.

10.8 The Act says that the other provisions of a pension scheme have effect subject to the non-discrimination rule explained above. This means that where there is a conflict between the non-discrimination rule and a rule of the pension scheme, the non-discrimination rule prevails. Thus, pension scheme trustees and managers do not have to act in accordance with a scheme rule which would produce a discriminatory result. The Act also ensures that pension scheme trustees and managers have power to make alterations to the scheme in order to make the scheme conform with the non-discrimination rule.

> The rules of an employer's final salary scheme provide that the maximum pension receivable by a member is equivalent to 2/3 of salary in the last year of work. An employee becomes disabled and as a result has to reduce her working hours for the remainder of her working life, which will amount to two years. She has worked for twenty years full time prior to this. The scheme's rules put the disabled person at a substantial disadvantage because, regardless of her previous twenty years' service, her pension will only be calculated on her part-time salary as a result of her disability. The trustees decide in her case to average out her salary over a period of years prior to her retirement date, which will enable her full-time earnings to be taken into account. This is likely to be a reasonable adjustment to make.

10.9 The duty to make reasonable adjustments applies to pension scheme trustees and managers in the same way as it applies to an employer. The duty is owed to disabled people who are members or prospective members of the scheme, and relates to any provision, criterion or practice (including a scheme rule) applied by or on behalf of the trustees or managers and any physical feature of premises which they occupy. The Act refers to making alterations to the rules of the pension scheme as an example of a reasonable adjustment.

10.10 Although the statutory non-discrimination rule does not apply in relation to rights accrued and benefits payable in respect of periods of service prior to 1 October 2004, it does apply to communications about such rights or benefits with members or prospective members of the scheme. So far as communications generally are concerned, both the non-discrimination rule and the duty to make reasonable adjustments apply in relation to disabled people who are entitled to, and currently receiving, dependants' or survivors' benefits under a pension scheme as they do in relation to disabled pensioner members of the scheme. The same applies in respect of pension credit members of the scheme. Communications include the provision of information and the operation of a dispute resolution procedure, and reasonable adjustments could involve providing information in accessible formats (such as large print, Braille, tape or disc), or providing a sign language interpreter for a meeting.

s 4G(4) & s 4K

> A blind woman whose partner dies and who is in receipt of a survivor's pension asks for and receives information about the pension scheme on tape. The information relates to the period before October 2004 but nevertheless this is likely to be a reasonable adjustment to make.

10

s 17A(1)   10.11   The Act says that if a disabled person believes that he has been unlawfully discriminated against in relation to an occupational pension scheme, he may make an application to an employment tribunal. This is the case whether the allegation of discrimination is made against the employer or against the trustees or managers of the pension scheme. Chapter 13 gives more information about making a claim under Part 2. However, the Act contains additional provisions which apply specifically to complaints relating to occupational pension schemes. These provisions are explained in the following paragraphs.

s 4I   10.12   When a disabled member or prospective member of an occupational pension scheme complains to an employment tribunal that he has been treated unlawfully under Part 2 by the trustees or managers of the scheme, the employer is treated as a party to the proceedings. The employer is therefore entitled to appear at the tribunal hearing and to make representations to the tribunal. This is because the employer may be required (as a matter of obligation or practice) to fund any award made against the trustees or managers of the scheme.

s 4J(1)   10.13   In addition, special rules may apply in respect of the remedies available when a complaint brought by a disabled person against the trustees or managers (or a complaint against the employer itself) is successful. Provided that the complainant is not a pensioner member of the scheme, these rules will apply to such a complaint if it relates to:

10

- the terms on which people become members of an occupational pension scheme, or

- the terms on which members of the scheme are treated.

10.14 In such circumstances, the Act modifies the usual rules governing the remedies which may be granted by an employment tribunal when it upholds a complaint (see paragraphs 13.14 to 13.16). In particular: s 4J(2) - (4)

- the tribunal may make a declaration that the complainant has a right to be admitted to the scheme or to membership of the scheme without discrimination in respect of a specified period, but

- the only compensation which the tribunal may award is compensation for injury to feelings and compensation of the kind described in paragraph 13.16.

10.15 A complaint about discrimination by pension scheme trustees or managers may also be made through the pensions dispute resolution mechanism which every occupational pension scheme is required to have for resolving disputes between individual pension scheme members and the trustees or managers. Information about the scheme should give details about this. The Pensions Ombudsman also has power to investigate complaints in certain circumstances. Details about the Pensions Ombudsman, and about the Pensions Advisory Service (which can provide an advice and conciliation service for members of the public who have problems with their occupational pensions), are given in Appendix C.

10

Group insurance services

s 4(2)
s 4A(1)

What does the Act say about employers?

10.16 As far as employers are concerned, Part 2 does not distinguish between discrimination in providing benefits relating to insurance and discrimination in relation to other benefits. Thus, an employer must not discriminate against a disabled person in the opportunities it affords him for receiving insurance-related benefits, or by refusing him, or deliberately not affording him, any such opportunity. The duty to make reasonable adjustments applies to the manner in which employers make insurance services available to a disabled employee. However, it should be noted that the employer's role is often limited to explaining the availability of group insurance services and to proposing employees to the insurer for cover under a group policy.

What does the Act say about group insurers?

s 18

10.17 The Act says that, where an insurer agrees with an employer to provide insurance services to its employees, or to give its employees an opportunity to receive such services, it is unlawful for the insurer to discriminate against a disabled person:

- who is an employee of that employer and who, by virtue of his employment, would ordinarily be eligible to receive such services, or

- who has applied for, or is contemplating applying for, such employment.

s 18(3)

10.18 The insurance services to which these principles apply are those for the provision of benefits in respect of:

- termination of service

- retirement, old age or death, or

- accident, injury, sickness or invalidity.

When does a group insurer discriminate against a disabled person?

10.19 Although discrimination by **employers** in providing insurance-related benefits is defined in the usual way for the purposes of Part 2 (as explained in Chapter 4), the circumstances in which **insurers** will be in breach of Part 2 are defined differently. For the purposes of Part 2, an insurer is only taken to discriminate against a disabled person if it acts in a way which would amount to discrimination under Part 3 (which deals with discrimination by the providers of goods, facilities or services). For this purpose, the insurer's actions have to be assessed as if the insurer were providing the service in question to members of the public, and as if the disabled person were receiving the service (or trying to secure its provision) as a member of the public.

s 18(2)

10.20 Part 3 makes it unlawful to discriminate against a disabled person for a disability-related reason in respect of the provision of goods, facilities or services to members of the public unless the conduct can be justified: for example, by reference to actuarial evidence. However, within the confines of the Code it is not possible to explain the operation of Part 3 in detail. The DRC has issued a separate code of practice giving guidance in this regard (see Appendix C for details).

10

s 17A(1)

10.21 The Act says that if a disabled person believes that he has been unlawfully discriminated against in relation to group insurance services, he may make an application to an employment tribunal. This is the case whether the allegation of discrimination is made against the employer or against the group insurer. Chapter 13 gives more information about making a claim under Part 2.

10

11 Discrimination in providing employment services

Introduction

11.1 Although the operation of Part 3 of the Act is mentioned in Chapter 10 (in the context of group insurance services), the explanation of the law in other chapters of the Code is confined to the Act's provisions on employment and occupation – which are in Part 2. However, as the purpose of the Code is to give practical guidance on how to prevent discrimination against disabled people in employment or when seeking employment, it is also necessary to look at what the Act says about the provision of employment services. Such services are covered by Part 3, which relates to discrimination in the provision of goods, facilities or services.

11.2 It is not the purpose of this chapter to give a detailed explanation of how the provisions of Part 3 work – but simply to summarise their application to employment services. For a full explanation of the operation of Part 3, reference should be made to the separate code of practice (the Part 3 Code) issued by the DRC in this regard (see Appendix C for details).

What are employment services?

11.3 For the purposes of Part 3, 'employment services' are:

s 21A(1)

■ vocational guidance or training services, or

■ services designed to assist people to find or keep jobs, or to establish themselves in an occupation in a self-employed capacity.

11.4 Employment services therefore include services provided by an employment agency or employment business. This includes employment services provided by Jobcentre Plus and other schemes that assist people to find work. Many people who receive employment services (or who seek the provision of such services) are engaged in, or seeking, contract work. This is particularly true of people who look for work by using the services of employment businesses. The Act gives rights to disabled contract workers not only in relation to the provision of employment services, but also in relation to the contract work itself. What the Act says about contract workers is explained in paragraphs 9.3 to 9.13.

What is unlawful under the Act?

Discrimination in providing employment services

s 19 applied by s 21A(4)

11.5 Where a person or body is concerned with the provision of employment services to the public, or a section of the public, the Act says that it is unlawful for it to discriminate against a disabled person:

- by refusing to provide (or deliberately not providing) to the disabled person any such service which it provides (or is prepared to provide) to members of the public

> An employment agency refuses to allow a disabled person with a mobility impairment to register with the agency as it says that it does not have any posts which would be 'suitable' and on the ground floor. This is likely to be unlawful.

- in the standard of service which it provides to the disabled person or the manner in which it provides the service

A temp agency which has a person with a hearing impairment on its books, does not contact him with any work, despite the fact that there is plenty of suitable work for him to do. This is likely to be unlawful.

A woman who has cerebral palsy visits a careers guidance service. The advisor is dismissive of various professions that the woman expresses an interest in, saying that they would be too difficult for her to get into because of her disability. This is likely to be unlawful.

- in the terms on which it provides the service to the disabled person.

A disabled person with a speech impairment requests job advice from his local careers guidance service. He is asked to return next week when there is more time available to meet his needs, although other people, who do not have speech impairments, are being seen there and then. This is likely to be unlawful.

11.6 It is irrelevant whether or not a charge is made for the provision of the service. More detailed guidance on the kinds of treatment which are unlawful in relation to the provision of services is set out in Chapter 3 of the Part 3 Code.

11.7 It is also unlawful for a provider of employment services to discriminate against a disabled person:

- in failing to comply with a duty to make reasonable adjustments (under section 21 of the Act) to a practice, policy or procedure in circumstances in which the effect of that failure is to place the disabled person at a substantial disadvantage in comparison with people who are not disabled in relation to the provision of the service

- in failing to comply with a duty to make reasonable adjustments (under section 21 of the Act) in relation to a physical feature in circumstances in which the effect of that failure is to make it impossible or unreasonably difficult for the disabled person to make use of any such service, or

- in failing to comply with a duty under that section to provide an auxiliary aid or service in the same circumstances.

The duties to make reasonable adjustments under section 21 are explained in paragraphs 11.15 to 11.19.

Harassment

s21A(2) 11.8 It is unlawful for a provider of employment services to subject a disabled person to harassment if that person is someone to whom such services are being provided, or who has requested such services from the provider.

> A disabled man who has autism visits a careers guidance service. The advisor makes offensive comments about the man's communication skills. This is likely to amount to harassment whether or not the advisor knows that the man has autism.

Victimisation

11.9 It is also unlawful for a provider of employment services to victimise a person (whether or not he is disabled).

s 55

Other unlawful acts

11.10 The provisions which apply under Part 2 in respect of relationships which have come to an end apply equally in respect of employment services, as do the provisions in respect of discriminatory advertisements. In addition, the sanctions which apply under Part 2 in respect of unlawful instructions or pressure to discriminate apply in respect of similar conduct relating to employment services.

ss 16A - 16C

What amounts to discrimination?

11.11 The Act says that, in the circumstances described in paragraphs 11.5 and 11.7, discrimination can occur in different ways.

s 20 applied by s 21A(5)

11.12 One way in which discrimination occurs is when treatment of a disabled person by a provider of employment services:

- is for a reason related to his disability

- the treatment is less favourable than the way in which the service provider treats (or would treat) others to whom that reason does not (or would not) apply, and

- the service provider cannot show that the treatment is justified.

11.13 Discrimination also occurs when a provider of such services fails to comply with a duty to make reasonable adjustments to a practice, policy or procedure.

11

11.14 In addition, discrimination occurs when a provider of employment services:

■ fails to comply with a duty to make reasonable adjustments in relation to a physical feature or a duty to provide an auxiliary aid or service, and

■ cannot show that the failure is justified.

What is the duty to make reasonable adjustments?

s 21

11.15 The duty to make reasonable adjustments under Part 3 requires service providers to take positive steps to make their services accessible to disabled people. What is required is set out in section 21, and comprises a series of duties falling into three main areas:

■ changing practices, policies and procedures (such as a policy of not admitting assistance dogs)

■ providing auxiliary aids and services (such as information in accessible formats)

■ overcoming a physical feature (such as stairs) by

    a. removing the feature, or

    b. altering it, or

    c. avoiding it, or

    d. providing services by alternative methods.

s 21
applied by
s 21A(6)

11.16 Where employment services are offered to the public, the provider of those services may have to make a reasonable adjustment if:

■ it has a practice, policy or procedure (including a provision or criterion) which places disabled people at a substantial disadvantage in comparison with people who are not disabled in relation to the provision of the service, or

- a physical feature makes it impossible or unreasonably difficult for disabled people to make use of such a service, or

- an auxiliary aid or service (such as information on tape or a sign language interpreter) would enable (or make it easier for) disabled people to make use of any such service.

11.17 To comply with the duty in these circumstances, the steps which the service provider has to take are those which it is reasonable, in all the circumstances of the case, for it to take in order to:

- change the practice, policy or procedure so that it no longer places disabled people at a substantial disadvantage

A vocational guidance organisation has a policy of not allowing dogs in its building. It would be reasonable to waive this policy so that disabled people with assistance dogs can enter the building.

- overcome the physical feature

A building from which an employment agency operates has no colour contrast on the entrance steps, making it unreasonably difficult for blind and partially sighted people to use them. It is likely to be reasonable to apply colour contrast to the steps.

- provide the auxiliary aid or service.

> A woman who has dyslexia finds it difficult to fill in an employment agency's registration form. An employee of the agency helps her to fill it in.

11.18 In contrast to the position under Part 2, a service provider's duty to make reasonable adjustments under Part 3 is a duty owed to disabled people at large. It is not simply a duty that is weighed up in relation to each individual disabled person who wants to access a service provider's services. Providers of employment services should therefore consider the need for reasonable adjustments in advance of being approached by a disabled person. Carrying out an access audit of their premises and services (including websites) is likely to assist service providers in this regard. More information about access audits and website accessibility is given in Appendix C.

> A recruitment agency advertises job vacancies on its website. The agency has its website checked for accessibility, and makes changes to enable disabled people using a variety of access software to use it.

11.19 More detailed guidance on the application of the duty to service providers is set out in Chapters 4 and 5 of the Part 3 Code. Chapter 6 of that Code gives guidance on how leases, building regulations and other statutory requirements affect a service provider's duty to make reasonable adjustments to premises. The issues are similar to (but not exactly the same as) those explained in the following chapter of this Code.

Can acts which are potentially discriminatory ever be justified?

11.20 Most conduct which is potentially unlawful under the Act is incapable of being justified. Treatment of a disabled person by a provider of employment services can never be justified if it amounts to direct discrimination (see paragraph 4.5), and the same applies to a failure to comply with a duty to make reasonable adjustments to a practice, policy or procedure. However, as noted at paragraphs 11.12 and 11.14, a provider of such services may in limited circumstances be permitted to justify certain other failures to make a reasonable adjustment as well as treatment which would otherwise amount to disability-related discrimination (see paragraph 11.21).

s 20(3A) applied by s 21A(5)

11.21 Where a claim of discrimination against a provider of employment services is based on a failure to comply with a duty to make reasonable adjustments in relation to a physical feature or a duty to provide an auxiliary aid or service, or on less favourable treatment which does not amount to direct discrimination, that failure or treatment (as the case may be) may be justified if:

s 20 applied by s 21A(5)

- the service provider holds the opinion that one or more of the conditions listed in section 20 of the Act are satisfied, and

- it is reasonable in all the circumstances of the case for it to hold that opinion.

11.22 The conditions listed in section 20 of the Act relate to:

- health or safety

- the disabled person being incapable of entering into a contract

11

- the service provider being otherwise unable to provide the service to the public

- enabling the service provider to provide the service to the disabled person or other members of the public, and

- the greater cost of providing a tailor-made service.

These conditions are explained in more detail in Chapter 7 of the Part 3 Code.

Bringing claims for discrimination relating to employment services

s 25(8)

11.23 The Act says that if a disabled person believes that he has been unlawfully discriminated against in respect of employment services, he may make an application to an employment tribunal. Discrimination includes victimisation, and employment tribunals also deal with claims of harassment in relation to employment services. This is an exception to the usual practice for claims brought under Part 3 – which are otherwise brought in a county court or, in Scotland, a sheriff court. Claims of discrimination in respect of employment services are therefore heard in the same venue as other employment-related discrimination claims.

12 Making reasonable adjustments to premises – legal considerations

Introduction

12.1 In Chapter 5 it was explained that one of the situations in which there is a duty to make reasonable adjustments arises where a physical feature of premises occupied by an employer places a disabled person at a substantial disadvantage compared with people who are not disabled. In such circumstances the employer must consider whether any reasonable steps can be taken to overcome that disadvantage. Making adjustments to premises may be a reasonable step for an employer to have to take. This applies equally to people or bodies other than employers who have duties under Part 2 of the Act. This chapter addresses the issues of how leases, building regulations and other statutory requirements affect the duty to make reasonable adjustments to premises.

12.2 The issues dealt with in this chapter largely concern the need to obtain consent to the making of reasonable adjustments where an employer occupies premises under a lease or other binding obligation. However, employers should remember that even where consent is not given for altering a physical feature, they still have a duty to make reasonable adjustments – which will involve them considering taking other steps to overcome the disadvantage which the feature causes in respect of the disabled person.

What about the need to obtain statutory consent for some building changes?

s 59

12.3 An employer might have to obtain statutory consent before making adjustments involving changes to premises. Such consents include planning permission, building regulations approval or a building warrant in Scotland, listed building consent, scheduled monument consent and fire regulations approval. The Act does not override the need to obtain such consents.

12.4 Employers should plan for and anticipate the need to obtain consent to make a particular adjustment. It might take time to obtain such consent, but it could be reasonable to make an interim or other adjustment – one that does not require consent – in the meantime.

> An employee who uses a wheelchair requires a ramp in order to access the building. The employer provides a temporary ramp, pending the outcome of an application for consent to install a permanent ramp. This is likely to be a reasonable step to take.

12.5 Where consent has been refused, there is likely to be a means of appeal. Whether or not the employer's duty to take such steps as it is reasonable to take includes pursuing an appeal will depend on the circumstances of the case.

Building Regulations and building design

SI 2000/2531

12.6 The design and construction of a new building, or the material alteration of an existing one, must comply with Building Regulations. For buildings in England or Wales, Part M of the Building Regulations (access to and use of buildings) is intended to ensure that reasonable provision is made for people to gain access to and use buildings. A similar provision applies in Scotland under the Technical Standards for compliance with the Building Standards (Scotland) Regulations 1990 and, from May 2005, under the Building (Scotland) Regulations 2004 and associated Technical Handbooks.

12.7 Nevertheless, the fact that the design and construction of a building (or a physical feature of a building) which an employer occupies meets the requirements of the Building Regulations does not diminish the employer's duty to make reasonable adjustments in respect of the building's physical features. In particular, it should be noted that the partial exemption from the duty to remove or alter physical features which applies to service providers under Part 3 of the Act does not apply to employers under Part 2.

12.8 The Building Regulations building standards provide only a baseline standard of accessibility, which is not intended to address the specific needs of individual employees. It is therefore good practice for employers to carry out an assessment of the access needs of each disabled employee, and to consider what alterations can be made to the features of its buildings in order to meet those needs. It is also good practice to anticipate the needs of disabled people when planning building or refurbishment works.

12.9 When assessing the access requirements of disabled people, it is likely to be helpful to refer to 'British Standard 8300:2001, Design of buildings and their approaches to meet the needs of disabled people – Code of Practice'. Indeed, it is unlikely to be reasonable for an employer to have to make an adjustment to a physical feature of a building which it occupies if the design and construction of the physical features of the

12

building is in accordance with BS8300. Further information about BS8300 can be found in Appendix C.

12.10 In addition, although less comprehensive than BS8300, guidance accompanying the Building Regulations (known as 'Approved Document M') sets out a number of 'provisions' as suggested ways in which the requirements of the Regulations might be met. It is unlikely to be reasonable for an employer to have to make an adjustment to a physical feature of a building which it occupies if that feature accords with the relevant provisions of the most up to date version of Approved Document M.

12.11 Financial assistance may be available from Access to Work to help meet the cost of making reasonable adjustments to the physical features of a building which an employer occupies (see paragraph 8.19).

What if a binding obligation other than a lease prevents a building being altered?

s 18B(3)

12.12 The employer may be bound by the terms of an agreement or other legally binding obligation (for example, a mortgage, charge or restrictive covenant or, in Scotland, a feu disposition) under which it cannot alter the premises without someone else's consent. In these circumstances, the Act provides that it is always reasonable for the employer to have to request that consent, but that it is never reasonable for the employer to have to make an alteration before having obtained that consent.

A retailer builds his shop with the assistance of a bank loan. The loan is secured by way of a charge on the shop under which the bank's consent is required for any changes. It is reasonable for the retailer to seek the bank's consent for changes (such as the installation of a lift) but it is not reasonable for the retailer to have to make any alterations if the bank does not give its consent.

What happens if a lease says that certain changes to premises cannot be made?

12.13 Special provisions apply where an employer occupies premises under a lease, the terms of which prevent it from making an alteration to the premises. In such circumstances, if the alteration is one which the employer proposes to make in order to comply with a duty of reasonable adjustment, the Act overrides the terms of the lease so as to entitle the employer to make the alteration with the consent of its landlord ('the lessor'). In such a case the employer must first write to the lessor asking for consent to make the alteration. The lessor cannot unreasonably withhold consent but may attach reasonable conditions to the consent.

s 18A(2)

12.14 If the employer fails to make a written application to the lessor for consent to the alteration, the employer will not be able to rely upon the fact that the lease has a term preventing it from making alterations to the premises to defend its failure to make an alteration. In these circumstances, anything in the lease which prevents that alteration being made must be ignored in deciding whether it was reasonable for the employer to have made the alteration.

Sch 4, Part I, para 1

12

An employer occupies premises under a lease a term of which says that the employer cannot make alterations to a staircase. When deciding whether or not it was reasonable for the employer to make an alteration to the staircase to overcome a disadvantage experienced by a disabled employee, a tribunal will ignore the term of the lease unless the employer has written to the lessor to ask for permission to make the alteration.

What happens if the lessor has a 'superior' lessor?

12.15 The employer's lessor may itself hold a lease the terms of which prevent it from consenting to the alteration without the consent of its landlord ('the superior lessor'). In such circumstances the effect of the superior lease is modified so as to require the lessee of that lease to apply in writing to its lessor (the 'superior lessor' in this context) if it wishes to consent to the alteration. As with the employer's lessor, the superior lessor must not withhold such consent unreasonably but may attach reasonable conditions to the consent.

A bank occupies its premises under a lease, the terms of which prevent it from making alterations without the consent of the landlord. The landlord holds the premises under a lease which has a similar term. The landlord receives an application from the bank for consent to alter the premises. The landlord is entitled to consent to the application if it receives the consent of its landlord. The bank's landlord writes to the superior lessor asking for this consent. The superior lessor cannot unreasonably refuse to give consent but may consent subject to reasonable conditions.

12.16 Where a superior lessor receives an application from its lessee, the provisions described in paragraphs 12.17 to 12.30 apply as if its lessee were the employer.

How do arrangements for gaining consent work?

12.17 Regulations made under the Act govern the procedure for obtaining consent. These Regulations (the Disability Discrimination (Employment Field) (Leasehold Premises) Regulations 2004) are referred to in this Chapter as the 'Leasehold Premises Regulations'.

SI 2004/153

12.18 The Leasehold Premises Regulations say that, once the application has been made, the lessor has 21 days, beginning with the day on which it receives the application, to reply in writing to the employer (or the person who made the application on its behalf). If it fails to do so it is taken to have unreasonably withheld its consent to the alteration. However, where it is reasonable to do so, the lessor is permitted to take more than 21 days to reply to the request.

reg 4

12.19 If the lessor replies consenting to the application subject to obtaining the consent of another person (required under a superior lease or because of a binding obligation), but fails to seek the consent of the other person within 21 days of receiving the application (or such longer period as may be reasonable), it will also be taken to have withheld its consent.

12.20 The Leasehold Premises Regulations provide that a lessor will be treated as not having sought the consent of another person unless the lessor has applied in writing to the other person indicating that the occupier has asked for consent for an

12

alteration in order to comply with a duty to make reasonable adjustments, and that the lessor has given its consent conditionally upon obtaining the other person's consent.

reg 6 12.21 If the lessor replies refusing consent to the alteration, the employer must inform the disabled person of this, but has no further obligation to make the alteration (but see paragraph 12.2).

When is it unreasonable for a lessor to withhold consent?

12.22 Whether withholding consent will be reasonable or not will depend on the specific circumstances. For example, if a particular adjustment is likely to result in a substantial permanent reduction in the value of the lessor's interest in the premises, the lessor is likely to be acting reasonably in withholding consent. The lessor is also likely to be acting reasonably if it withholds consent because an adjustment would cause significant disruption or inconvenience to other tenants (for example, where the premises consist of multiple adjoining units).

A particular adjustment helps make a public building more accessible generally and is therefore likely to benefit the landlord. It is likely to be unreasonable for consent to be withheld in these circumstances.

A particular adjustment is likely to result in a substantial permanent reduction in the value of the landlord's interest in the premises. The landlord is likely to be acting reasonably in withholding consent.

A particular adjustment would cause significant disruption or major inconvenience to other tenants (for example, where the premises consist of multiple adjoining units). The landlord is likely to be acting reasonably in withholding consent.

12.23 A trivial or arbitrary reason would almost certainly be unreasonable. Many reasonable adjustments to premises will not harm the lessor's interests and so it would generally be unreasonable to withhold consent for them.

12.24 The Leasehold Premises Regulations say that, provided the consent has been sought in the way required by the lease, it is unreasonable for a lessor to withhold consent in circumstances where the lease says that consent will be given to alterations of the kind for which consent has been sought.

reg 5

12.25 The Leasehold Premises Regulations provide that withholding consent will be reasonable where:

reg 6

- there is a binding obligation requiring the consent of any person to the alteration

- the lessor has taken steps to seek consent, and

- consent has not been given or has been given subject to a condition making it reasonable for the lessor to withhold its consent.

It will also be reasonable for a lessor to withhold consent where it is bound by an agreement under which it would have to make a payment in order to give the consent, but which prevents it from recovering the cost from the employer.

12

What conditions would it be reasonable for a lessor to make when giving consent?

12.26 The Leasehold Premises Regulations set out some conditions which it is reasonable for a lessor to make. Depending on the circumstances of the case there may be other conditions which it would also be reasonable for a lessor to require the employer to meet. Where a lessor imposes other conditions, their reasonableness may be challenged in the course of subsequent employment tribunal proceedings (see paragraph 12.28).

reg 7

12.27 The conditions set out in the Leasehold Premises Regulations as ones which a lessor may reasonably require an employer to meet are that it:

- obtains any necessary planning permission and other statutory consents

- submits plans and specifications for the lessor's approval (provided that such approval will not be unreasonably withheld) and thereafter carries out the work in accordance with them

- allows the lessor a reasonable opportunity to inspect the work after it is completed, or

- reimburses the lessor's reasonable costs incurred in connection with the giving of consent.

In addition, in a case where it would be reasonable for the lessor to withhold consent, the lessor may give such consent subject to a condition that the premises are reinstated to their original condition at the end of the lease.

What happens if the lessor refuses consent or attaches conditions to consent?

12.28 Where a disabled person brings legal proceedings against his employer under Part 2 – and those proceedings involve a failure to make an alteration to premises – he may ask the employment tribunal hearing the case to bring in the lessor as an additional party to the proceedings. The employer may also make such a request. The tribunal will grant that request if it is made before the hearing of the case begins. It may refuse the request if it is made after the hearing of the claim begins. The request will not be granted if it is made after the tribunal has determined the claim.

Sch 4, Part I, para 2

12.29 Where the lessor has been made a party to the proceedings, the employment tribunal may determine whether the lessor has unreasonably refused consent to the alteration or has consented subject to unreasonable conditions. In either case, the tribunal can:

- make an appropriate declaration

- make an order authorising the employer to make a specified alteration

- order the lessor to pay compensation to the disabled person.

12.30 The tribunal may require the employer to comply with any conditions specified in the order. If the tribunal orders the lessor to pay compensation, it cannot also order the employer to do so.

Comparison with the procedure for obtaining consent under Part 3

12.31 There are similar provisions which govern the procedure by which a service provider may obtain

12

consent to an alteration which it proposes to make in order to comply with a duty of reasonable adjustment under Part 3 of the Act. These provisions – which are explained in Chapter 6 of the Part 3 Code – apply where a provider of employment services needs to obtain consent in order to make a reasonable adjustment (see paragraphs 11.16 and 11.17). However, it should be noted that the procedures for obtaining consent under Parts 2 and 3 differ in certain ways. In particular:

- The periods within which the lessor must respond to an application for consent are not the same – under Part 3 the relevant period is 42 days beginning with the day on which the application is received

- Under Part 3 the lessor may require plans and specifications to be submitted **before** it decides whether to give consent

- Under Part 3 it is possible to make a free-standing reference to the court if the lessor has either refused consent or attached conditions to it. Under Part 2, the question of consent to alterations can only be considered by an employment tribunal in the course of a complaint of discrimination.

13 Other relevant provisions

13.1 Additional provisions of the Act (and provisions of other legislation) are relevant to understanding the protection from discrimination afforded to disabled people in respect of employment. This chapter describes those provisions, and focuses in particular on the way in which disputes should be resolved.

Resolving disputes

When is it necessary to try to resolve disputes within the workplace?

13.2 It is good practice to attempt to resolve disputes within the workplace and without resorting to legal proceedings. In addition, legislation **requires** employers and employees to try to do this in certain circumstances. The requirement may apply where an employer has dismissed an employee, or is contemplating dismissing him, or taking disciplinary action against him, or where an employee has a grievance against his employer. In broad terms, the statutory procedures – which are set out in the Employment Act 2002 (the 2002 Act) – require:

- the grounds for the employer's action, or details of the employee's grievance, to be set out in writing and sent to the other party

- a meeting to take place between the employer and employee in order to discuss the matter, and for the employer to inform the employee of its decision afterwards, and

- an internal appeal against that decision to take place if the employee is not satisfied with it.

13.3 Employers must make reasonable adjustments in respect of the way in which the statutory procedures are implemented to prevent a disabled person from being placed at a substantial disadvantage in comparison with people who are not disabled. Failure to do so will itself amount to a breach of the 1995 Act.

13.4 So, for example, it is likely to be a reasonable adjustment for an employer to allow a disabled employee who has communication difficulties some assistance to make a written statement of a grievance he wishes to make (such as by providing him with assistance via a non-interested party). Depending on the circumstances, it may be reasonable to allow a disabled person with learning disabilities to be accompanied to a meeting by a family member or friend, or to send written communications to a blind or visually impaired person in a format which is accessible to him.

13.5 The effect of what the 2002 Act says about dispute resolution is that, where an employee has a grievance against his employer (including an allegation that the employer has breached Part 2 of the 1995 Act), he may not commence employment tribunal proceedings without first giving the employer a written statement of the reasons for the grievance.

13.6 In addition, in any employment tribunal proceedings where it appears to the tribunal that the statutory procedures apply, any award which the tribunal makes will be either reduced or increased if the procedures were not fully complied with before the proceedings were begun. The award will be reduced if the tribunal concludes that the failure to comply is wholly or mainly attributable to the employee. It will be increased if the tribunal concludes that the employer is wholly or mainly at fault. Save in exceptional circumstances, the amount by which any award will be reduced or increased will be between 10% and 50%.

13.7 Although, as stated above, it is good practice to try to resolve disputes within the workplace wherever possible, there are occasions where internal dispute resolution will not be practical or appropriate. The legislation recognises this, and the statutory procedures mentioned in paragraph 13.2 do not have to be complied with in respect of every claim which arises under Part 2.

13.8 Compliance with those procedures is only **required** in respect of disputes involving employers and employees who work (or have worked) under a contract of service or apprenticeship. People who fall within the wider definition of 'employment' set out at paragraph 3.8 do not need to use the statutory procedures before bringing a claim in the employment tribunal. Neither do those procedures apply to disputes under the Act involving partners in firms, barristers or advocates, or office holders, for example. Equally, they do not apply in respect of disputes between employees and pension scheme trustees or managers, or to disputes involving providers of employment services.

13.9 As indicated above, however, there are also cases where, because of the circumstances surrounding the dispute, it may be inappropriate for the parties to be required to seek a resolution within the workplace. The Employment Act 2002 (Dispute Resolution) Regulations 2004 (the 2004

SI 2004/752 reg 11

13

Regulations) provide that the statutory procedures do not need to be followed if:

- one of the parties to the dispute has reasonable grounds to believe that compliance with the procedure would result in a significant threat to himself, his property or another person, or

- one of the parties has been subjected to harassment and has reasonable grounds to believe that complying with the procedure would result in his being subjected to further harassment, or

- it is not practicable to comply with the procedure within a reasonable period.

reg 7 13.10 In addition, the 2004 Regulations say that, where an employee's grievance is that disciplinary action taken against him itself amounts to discrimination by the employer, the parties are not required to meet to discuss the matter. However, an employee must still send the employer written details of his grievance before commencing employment tribunal proceedings.

What if a dispute cannot be resolved by using an employer's grievance procedure?

s 17A(1)
s 55
13.11 The Act says that a person who believes that someone has unlawfully discriminated against him (which includes victimising him or failing to make a reasonable adjustment) or has subjected him to harassment, may make an application to **Sch 3,** an employment tribunal. Such an application **para 3** must normally be made within three months of the date when the incident complained about occurred. Before making an application to a tribunal, however, it is necessary to ensure that any requirement under the 2002 Act relating to

13

internal dispute resolution procedures has been complied with (see paragraphs 13.2 to 13.10).

13.12 In cases where such a procedure applies, the 2004 Regulations say that the usual time limit is extended by three months (so that the time limit for making a claim becomes six months in total). However, this only applies to those people who are **required** to use such a procedure. It does not apply to people who do not have to do so (see paragraph 13.8).

reg 15

13.13 Before making an application to an employment tribunal (or within 28 days of lodging it), a disabled person can request information relevant to his claim from the person against whom the claim is made. This is known as the 'questionnaire procedure'. There is a standard form of questionnaire (DL56) and accompanying booklet which explains how the procedure works (see Appendix C for details).

13.14 When an application to an employment tribunal has been made, a conciliation officer from the Advisory, Conciliation and Arbitration Service (ACAS) will try to promote settlement of the dispute without a tribunal hearing. However, if a hearing becomes necessary – and if the application is upheld – the tribunal may:

s 17A(2)

- declare the rights of the disabled person (the applicant), and the other person (the respondent) in relation to the application

- order the respondent to pay the applicant compensation, and

- recommend that, within a specified time, the respondent takes reasonable action to prevent or reduce the adverse effect in question.

s 17A(4)   13.15 The Act allows compensation for injury to feelings to be awarded whether or not other compensation is awarded.

s 17A(5)   13.16 The Act also says that if a respondent fails, without reasonable justification, to comply with an employment tribunal's recommendation, the tribunal may:

- increase the amount of compensation to be paid, or

- order the respondent to pay compensation if it did not make such an order earlier.

s 4J   13.17 It should be noted that in relation to certain claims of discrimination concerning occupational pension schemes, the Act modifies the remedies available (see paragraphs 10.13 and 10.14).

13.18 Sources of information about how to make an application to an employment tribunal are listed in Appendix C.

Other provisions

Anti-avoidance provisions

Sch 3A, Part 1   13.19 Generally speaking, a disabled person cannot waive his rights (or an employer's duties) under the Act. The Act says that any term in a contract of employment or other agreement is 'void' (i.e. not valid) where:

- making the contract is unlawful under Part 2 because of the inclusion of the term

- the term is included in furtherance of an act which is itself unlawful under Part 2, or

- the term provides for the doing of an act which is unlawful under Part 2.

13

13.20 An employer should not include in an agreement any provision intended to avoid obligations under the Act, or to prevent someone from fulfilling obligations. An agreement should not, therefore, be used to try to justify less favourable treatment or deem an adjustment unreasonable. Even parts of agreements which unintentionally have such an effect are unenforceable if they would restrict the working of the Act's provisions on employment and occupation. However, as explained in Chapter 12, special arrangements cover leases and other agreements which might restrict the making of adjustments to premises.

Compromise agreements

13.21 The effect of the Act's provisions is also to make a contract term unenforceable if it would prevent anyone from making an application to an employment tribunal under Part 2, or would force them to discontinue an application (see paragraph 13.11). There is a limited exception to this principle relating to settlement agreements which have either been brokered by an ACAS conciliation officer, or which are made in circumstances where the following conditions are satisfied:

Sch 3A, Part 1

- the disabled person has received advice from a relevant independent adviser about the terms and effects of the agreement, particularly its effect on his ability to apply to a tribunal

- the adviser has a contract of insurance or an indemnity provided for members of a profession or professional body, and

- the agreement is in writing, relates to the application, identifies the adviser and says that these conditions are satisfied.

13

The Act defines the circumstances in which a person is a 'relevant independent adviser' for this purpose.

Variation of contracts

13.22 A disabled person interested in a contract of employment or other agreement which contains a term of the kind mentioned in paragraph 13.19 may apply to a county court or, in Scotland, a sheriff court, for an order removing or modifying that term.

Collective agreements and rules of undertakings

13.23 There are also anti-avoidance provisions in the Act relating to the terms of collective agreements, and to rules made by employers in relation to working practices or recruitment. The Act says that any such term or rule is void where:

- making the collective agreement is unlawful under Part 2 because of the inclusion of the term

- the term or rule is included in furtherance of an act which is itself unlawful under Part 2, or

- the term or rule provides for the doing of an act which is unlawful under Part 2.

13.24 It does not matter whether the collective agreement was entered into, or the rule was made, before or after these provisions became law – the term or rule in question can still be challenged under the Act. In addition, where these provisions apply, certain disabled people may ask an employment tribunal to make a declaration that a discriminatory term or rule is void if they believe that it may affect them in the future. The Act specifies which disabled people may make such an application.

13

13.25 Although the Act does not prevent posts being advertised as open only to disabled candidates, there is a requirement under section 7 of the Local Government and Housing Act 1989 that every appointment to local authorities must be made on merit. This means that a post cannot be advertised by a local authority employer as open only to disabled people. Applications from disabled people can nevertheless be encouraged. In addition, this requirement to appoint 'on merit' does not exclude the duty under the 1995 Act to make reasonable adjustments. A disabled person's 'merit' must therefore be assessed after taking into account any such adjustments.

Provision for certain charities

13.26 The Act says that some charities (and government-funded supported employment – such as Workstep) are allowed to treat some groups of disabled people more favourably than others. But they can do this only if two conditions are met. First, the group being treated more favourably must be connected with the charitable purposes of the charity. Second, the more favourable treatment of that group must be in pursuance of those charitable purposes. In the case of supported employment, those treated more favourably must be disabled people whom the programme aims to help.

s 18C

Disability Rights Commission

General functions

13.27 The DRC has statutory powers to work towards the elimination of discrimination and to promote the equalisation of opportunity for disabled people. In particular, the DRC:

Disability Rights Commission Act 1999

13

- keeps the Act under review

- supplies assistance and support to disabled litigants under the Act

- provides information and advice to anyone with rights or obligations under the Act

- carries out formal investigations, and

- prepares new or revised Codes of Practice.

Enforcement of certain provisions under Part 2

13.28 In addition, the DRC has a direct involvement in the enforcement of the provisions of Part 2 relating to:

- instructing or pressurising other people to act unlawfully (see paragraph 3.22), and

- discriminatory advertisements (see paragraphs 7.12 and 7.13).

s 17B 13.29 Only the DRC may bring proceedings in respect of these matters. Where it does so, the DRC may seek:

- a declaration from an employment tribunal that a contravention has occurred, and

- an injunction from a county court (or, in Scotland, an order from a sheriff court) restraining further contraventions.

13.30 The DRC may only apply for an injunction or order if it has first obtained a declaration from an employment tribunal that an unlawful act has occurred, and then only if it appears to the DRC that a further unlawful act is likely to occur unless the person concerned is restrained.

13.31 The Commission may be contacted at:
DRC Information, Freepost, MID 02164, Stratford
upon Avon, CV37 9BR.

For other contact details, please see paragraph
1.21.

Appendix A: Changes to the Act

The table below summarises the main changes to the Act's provisions on employment and occupation taking effect on 1 October 2004. It does not include all the changes occurring on that date, and is not a full explanation of the law.

	Position before 1st October 2004
Scope	<ul><li>DDA covered employers with 15 or more employees.</li><li>Some occupations (e.g. police & firefighters) were not covered.</li></ul>
Types of Discrimination	Three kinds of discrimination:<ul><li>Less favourable treatment.</li><li>Failure to make reasonable adjustments.</li><li>Victimisation.</li></ul>
When is Justification relevant?	Justification was of relevance in cases about:<ul><li>Less favourable treatment.</li><li>Failure to make reasonable adjustments.</li></ul>
Harassment	Covered, but no separate provisions on this.
Claims	Most claims covered by the Code were brought in the employment tribunal apart from those involving trustees and managers of occupational pension schemes and claims about employment services.

Position after 1st October 2004

- All employers are covered by the DDA except for the Armed Forces.
- New occupations such as police and partners in firms are covered.
- Practical work experience, whether paid or unpaid, is covered.
- There are new provisions on discriminatory advertisements.
- Employment services are covered.

Four kinds of discrimination:
- Direct discrimination.
- Failure to make reasonable adjustments.
- 'Disability-related discrimination'.
- Victimisation.

Justification is NOT relevant in cases about:
- Direct discrimination.
- Failure to make reasonable adjustments.

Justification is relevant in cases about:
- Disability-related discrimination.

New provisions on harassment.

All claims covered by this Code are brought in the employment tribunal.

Appendix B: The meaning of disability

This appendix is included to aid understanding about who is covered by the Act and should provide sufficient information on the definition of disability to cover the large majority of cases. The definition of disability in the Act is designed to cover only people who would generally be considered to be disabled. A Government publication 'Guidance on matters to be taken into account in determining questions relating to the definition of disability', is also available.

When is a person disabled?

A person has a disability if he has a physical or mental impairment, which has a substantial and long-term adverse effect on his ability to carry out normal day-to-day activities.

What about people who have recovered from a disability?

People who have had a disability within the definition are protected from discrimination even if they have since recovered.

What does 'impairment' cover?

It covers physical or mental impairments; this includes sensory impairments, such as those affecting sight or hearing.

Are all mental impairments covered?

The term 'mental impairment' is intended to cover a wide range of impairments relating to mental functioning, including what are often known as learning disabilities. The Act says that a mental illness must be a clinically well-recognised illness in order to amount to a mental impairment. A clinically well-recognised illness is one that is recognised by a respected body of medical opinion.

What is a 'substantial' adverse effect?

A substantial adverse effect is something which is more than a minor or trivial effect. The requirement that an effect must be substantial reflects the general understanding of disability as a limitation going beyond the normal differences in ability which might exist among people.

What is a 'long-term' effect?

A long-term effect of an impairment is one:

- which has lasted at least 12 months, or

- where the total period for which it lasts is likely to be at least 12 months, or

- which is likely to last for the rest of the life of the person affected.

Effects which are not long-term would therefore include loss of mobility due to a broken limb which is likely to heal within 12 months and the effects of temporary infections, from which a person would be likely to recover within 12 months.

What if the effects come and go over a period of time?

If an impairment has had a substantial adverse effect on normal day-to-day activities but that effect ceases, the substantial effect is treated as continuing if it is likely to recur; that is if it is more probable than not that the effect will recur.

What are 'normal day-to-day activities'?

They are activities which are carried out by most people on a fairly regular and frequent basis. The term is not intended to include activities which are normal only for a particular person or group of people, such as playing a musical instrument, or a sport, to a professional standard or performing a skilled or specialised task at work. However, someone who is affected in such a specialised way but is also affected in normal day-to-day activities would be covered by this part of the definition. The test of whether an impairment affects normal day-to-day activities is whether it affects one of the broad categories of capacity listed in Schedule 1 to the Act. They are:

- mobility
- manual dexterity
- physical co-ordination
- continence
- ability to lift, carry or otherwise move everyday objects
- speech, hearing or eyesight
- memory or ability to concentrate, learn or understand, or
- perception of the risk of physical danger.

What about treatment?

Someone with an impairment may be receiving medical or other treatment which alleviates or removes the effects (though not the impairment). In such cases, the treatment is ignored and the impairment is taken to have the effect it would have had without such treatment. This does not apply if substantial adverse effects are not likely to recur even if the treatment stops (i.e. the impairment has been cured).

Does this include people who wear spectacles?

No. The sole exception to the rule about ignoring the effects of treatment is the wearing of spectacles or contact lenses. In this case, the effect while the person is wearing spectacles or contact lenses should be considered.

Are people who have disfigurements covered?

People with severe disfigurements are covered by the Act. They do not need to demonstrate that the impairment has a substantial adverse effect on their ability to carry out normal day-to-day activities.

What about people who know their condition is going to get worse over time?

Progressive conditions are conditions which are likely to change and develop over time. Examples given in the Act are cancer, multiple sclerosis, muscular dystrophy and HIV infection. Where a person has a progressive condition he will be covered by the Act from the moment the condition leads to an impairment which has some effect on ability to carry out normal day-to-day activities, even though not a substantial effect, if that impairment is likely eventually to have a substantial adverse effect on such ability.

What about people who are blind or partially sighted?

People who are registered as blind or partially sighted, or who are certified as being blind or partially sighted by a consultant ophthalmologist are automatically treated under the Act as being

SI 2003/712

disabled. People who are not registered or certified as blind or partially sighted will be covered by the Act if they can establish that they meet the Act's definition of disability.

Are people with genetic conditions covered?

If a genetic condition has no effect on ability to carry out normal day-to-day activities, the person is not covered. Diagnosis does not in itself bring someone within the definition. If the condition is progressive, then the rule about progressive conditions applies.

Are any conditions specifically excluded from the coverage of the Act?

Yes. Certain conditions are to be regarded as not amounting to impairments for the purposes of the Act. These are:

- addiction to or dependency on alcohol, nicotine, or any other substance (other than as a result of the substance being medically prescribed)

- seasonal allergic rhinitis (e.g. hayfever), except where it aggravates the effect of another condition

- tendency to set fires

- tendency to steal

- tendency to physical or sexual abuse of other persons

- exhibitionism

- voyeurism.

Also, disfigurements which consist of a tattoo (which has not been removed), non-medical body piercing, or something attached through such piercing, are to be treated as not having a substantial adverse effect on the person's ability to carry out normal day-to-day activities.

Appendix C: Further information

Online information

There is a wide range of practical information about employing disabled people and about the Disability Discrimination Act available free of charge on the DRC website.

Website: www.drc-gb.org

Leaflets about the Act

A range of leaflets about the Act is available online and can also be obtained free of charge from the DRC Helpline. Calls to the Helpline are charged at local rate.

Telephone: 08457 622 633

Textphone: 08457 622 644

Fax: 08457 778 878

Website: www.drc-gb.org

Post: DRC Helpline,
            FREEPOST,
            MID 02164,
            Stratford Upon Avon,
            CV37 9BR

The leaflets produced by the DRC include practical guides to the Act designed for disabled people and for employers. There is also a practical guide which is specifically intended to assist small employers.

Codes of Practice

Codes of Practice and accompanying guidance for Part 2 (this Code as well as the Code of Practice for Trade Organisations and Qualifications Bodies), Part 3 (Rights of access - Goods, facilities, services and premises) and Part 4 (Codes of practice for schools and post-16 education) are available through the DRC website (in electronic form) and through the Stationery Office on:

Telephone: 0870 600 5522

Fax: 0870 600 5533

Email: book.orders@tso.co.uk

Website: www.tso.co.uk

Guidance about making a claim

Employment tribunal application forms can be obtained from Jobcentre Plus offices and from Citizens' Advice Bureaux. The DRC also produces a self-help pack about making a claim in an employment tribunal. Information about the Questions Procedure is also available from the DRC. The forms DL56 and accompanying guidance can be obtained either through the DRC website or from the DRC Helpline.

Guidance on building design

Copies of BS8300 'Designing Buildings and their approaches to meet the access needs of disabled people' can be obtained from the British Standards Institute:

Telephone: 020 8996 9002

Fax: 020 8996 7001

Website: www.bsi-global.com

Access audits

The National Register of Access Consultants provides a database of registered access auditors.

Telephone: 020 7234 0434
Fax: 020 7357 8183
Minicom: 020 7357 8182
Email: info@nrac.org.uk
Website: www.nrac.org.uk

Making websites accessible

Disabled people use a wide range of specialist hardware and software to access computers. It is important that websites are designed to be compatible with this. Websites can also have 'access features' built into their design, such as a choice of font sizes or colour schemes.

RNIB's online Web Access Centre can provide more information on designing and evaluating websites.

Telephone: 020 7391 2178
Email: webaccess@rnib.org.uk
Website: www.rnib.org.uk

Health and Safety

The Health and Safety Commission (HSC) and the Health and Safety Executive (HSE) are responsible for the regulation of almost all the risks to health and safety arising from work activity in Britain.

Telephone: 08701 545500
Fax: 02920 859260
Minicom: 02920 808537
Email: hseinformationservices@natbrit.com
Website: www.hse.gov.uk

Jobcentre Plus (including Access to Work and the Disability Symbol)

There is a wide range of practical help and advice to assist employers in the recruitment and employment of disabled people available from Jobcentre Plus. Telephone numbers and addresses of local Jobcentre Plus offices can be found in local telephone directories or through the Jobcentre Plus website www.jobcentreplus.gov.uk

Jobcentre Plus also provides information and advice to disabled people in work or looking for work. It is a first point of contact for people wishing to get help from the Access to Work scheme. Disabled people should contact a Disability Employment Advisor at their local Jobcentre Plus office about Access to Work or about any other employment issues, whether they are in work or looking for work. Information about Access to Work can also be obtained from Access to Work business centres. Your local Access to Work business centre can be found through the Jobcentre Plus website www.jobcentreplus.gov.uk or by talking to a member of staff at a local Jobcentre Plus office. Jobcentre Plus can also provide employers with information about the Disability Symbol.

What does the Access to Work scheme offer?

Access to Work may be able to offer advice and help on the following:

Adaptations to premises and equipment

Modification of an employer's or self-employed person's premises or equipment, to enable them to employ or retain a disabled employee.

Employers will be expected to contribute if adaptations bring general benefits to the business, firm, other employees or customers.

Communication support at interview

Help with the costs of employing an interpreter or communicator to accompany a hearing impaired person, where there might be communication difficulties at a job interview with an employer.

Miscellaneous assistance

Provision under this element is predominantly in the form of one-off items of support that do not fit elsewhere, such as a grant towards the costs of deaf awareness training for close colleagues of a deaf person. Cost of travel **within** work is also placed in this element.

Special aids and equipment

Provision of aids and equipment to a disabled person which a non-disabled person doing the same job would not need. Leasing equipment can also be considered when it offers the most cost-effective solution. Employers will be expected to contribute if aids bring general benefits to the business, firm, other employees or customers.

Support workers

Help with the costs of employing personal support for a person with a disability at a job interview (e.g. advocacy support); on their journey to and from work (e.g. escort or driver) and help in the workplace including Personal Readers.

Travel to work

Support when a disabled person incurs extra costs in travelling to and from work because of their disability. Beneficiaries are expected to contribute the usual costs of travelling to work by public transport (or mileage costs where there is no public transport).

What is the Disability Symbol?

The Disability Symbol is a recognition given by Jobcentre Plus to employers who have agreed to take action to meet five commitments regarding the employment, retention, training and career development of disabled employees.

Employers who use the symbol have agreed with Jobcentre Plus that they will take action on these five commitments:

- to interview all disabled applicants who meet the minimum criteria for a job vacancy and consider them on their abilities

- to ensure there is a mechanism in place to discuss, at any time, but at least once a year, with disabled employees what can be done to make sure they can develop and use their abilities

- to make every effort when employees become disabled to make sure they stay in employment

- to take action to ensure that all employees develop the appropriate level of disability awareness needed to make these commitments work

- each year, to review the five commitments and what has been achieved, plan ways to improve on them and let employees and Jobcentre Plus know about progress and future plans.

Other sources of information

ACAS, the Advisory, Conciliation and Arbitration Service can help employers and individuals with information on legislation and on industrial relations practices and procedures. ACAS has a Helpline service which can be contacted on:

Telephone: 08457 47 47 47

Textphone: 08456 06 16 00

Website: www.acas.org.uk

Equality Direct also gives advice to employers across a range of equality issues (available in England only).

Telephone/Textphone: 08457 600 3444

Website: www.equalitydirect.org.uk

The Information Commissioner's Office provides information and guidance about the Data Protection Act and the Codes of Practice which relate to it.

Telephone: 01625 545 745

Fax: 01625 524510

Email: mail@ico.gsi.gov.uk

Website: www.informationcommissioner.gov.uk

The Pensions Ombudsman investigates and makes decisions about complaints and disputes about the way that occupational pension schemes are run.

Telephone: 020 7834 9144

Fax: 020 7821 0065

Email: enquiries@pensions-ombudsman.org.uk

Website: www.pensions-ombudsman.org.uk

OPAS, The Pensions Advisory Service, is an independent organisation that provides information and guidance on the whole spectrum of pensions, including State, company, personal and stakeholder schemes. It can help any member of the public who has a problem, complaint or dispute with their occupational or private pension provider.

Telephone: 0845 6012923

Fax: 020 7233 8016

Email: enquiries@opas.org.uk

Website: www.opas.org.uk

Index